THE STORY OF
THE ARK OF THE COVENANT

from Mount Sinai to Mount Moriah

The Story of the Ark of the Covenant by Hugo Bouter
Cover illustration: The Tabernacle in the Wilderness
Copyright © 2002 Chapter Two Trust, London

Originally published in Dutch in 1984
First English edition - 1988
Second edition - 1993
Third, revised edition - 2002

ISBN 1 85307 192 7 paperback
Printed in the Netherlands
Bible quotations are from the New King James Version

HUGO BOUTER

THE STORY OF
THE ARK
OF THE COVENANT

from Mount Sinai to Mount Moriah

CHAPTER TWO

FOUNTAIN HOUSE - CONDUIT MEWS, LONDON

Distributors:

• Bible, Book and Tract Depot, 23 Santa Rosa Avenue, Ryde, NSW 2112, Australia
• Bible House, Gateway Mall, 35 Tudor Street, Bridgetown, Barbados, WI
• Believers Bookshelf, 5205 Regional Road 81, Unit 3, Beamsville, ON, L0R 1B3, Canada
• Bible Treasury Bookstore Inc., 46 Queen Street, Dartmouth, NS, B2Y 1G1, Canada
• El-Ekhwa Library, 3 Anga Hanem Street, Shoubra, Cairo, Egypt
• Bibles & Publications Chrétiennes, 30 Rue Châteauvert, 26000 Valence, France
• CSV, An der Schloßfabrik 30, 42499 Hückeswagen, Germany
• Christian Truth Bookroom, Paddisonpet, Tenali 522 201, Andhra Pradesh, India
• Words of Life Trust, 3 Chuim, Khar, Mumbai 400 052, India
• Words of Truth, 38-P.D.A. Lamphelpat, Imphal 795 004, Manipur, India
• Uit het Woord der Waarheid, Postbox 260, 7120 AG Aalten, Netherlands
• Bible and Book Depot, Box 25119, Christchurch 5, New Zealand
• Christian Literature Depot, P.O. Box 436, Ijeshatedo, Surulere, Lagos, Nigeria
• Echoes of Truth, No 11 Post Office Road, P.O. Box 2637, Mushin, Lagos, Nigeria
• Kristen Litteratur, Elvebakkveien 9, 4270 Åkrehamn, Norway
• Grace & Truth Book-room, 87 Chausee Road, Castries, St. Lucia, WI
• Beröa Verlag, Zellerstraße 61, 8038 Zürich, Switzerland
• Dépôt de Bibles et Traités Chrétiens, 4 Rue du Nord, 1800 Vevey, Switzerland
• Chapter Two Bookshop, 199 Plumstead Common Road, London, SE18 2UJ, UK
• HoldFast Bible & Tract Depot, 100 Camden Road, Tunbridge Wells, Kent, TN1 2QP, UK
• Words of Truth, P.O. Box 147, Belfast, BT8 4TT, Northern Ireland, UK
• Believers Bookshelf Inc., Box 261, Sunbury, PA 17801, USA

"Arise, O LORD, to Your resting place,
You and the ark of Your strength".

Psalm 132:8

CONTENTS

PREFACE TO THE THIRD EDITION

The reason why the story of the ark of the covenant is so important is that the ark was the throne of God, His dwelling place in the midst of His people Israel from which He exercised His authority and His administration over them. Indissolubly connected with the ark is therefore the fact of God's **presence** in the midst of His chosen people.

The eventful story of the ark from Mount Sinai through the wilderness to the Promised Land, its crossing of the river Jordan, its wanderings in the land of Canaan, searching for its final resting place – all these events contain many important lessons and not least for the people of God in the present dispensation of grace. For it is here we are shown how the people of God behaved in the presence of God and also how God's enemies experienced His presence when they came in contact with it (and one especially thinks of the Philistines, who are a type of nominal Christians).

The events surrounding the ark present the following questions to us as Christians: What is our attitude towards God's presence amongst His own? Do we recognize His rights, and do we grant Him the central place that is due to Him?

Apart from a number of technical and textual changes this third edition is largely similar to the previous revised edition. May God graciously use the reading of this book for His own glory and the benefit of His children.

London, Spring 2002

"A mere journey from Egypt to Canaan would not have constituted true pilgrimage. Many a one had travelled that road without being a stranger and pilgrim with God... A merely toilsome, self-denying life, even though endued with that moral courage which becomes God's strangers on earth, will not do.

In order to make that journey the journey of God's Israel, the ark must be in their company, borne by a people ransomed by blood out of Egypt, and tending, in their faith of a promise, to Canaan... And what ark is in the midst of the saints now for safe and holy and honourable conduct through the desert world, if not the name of the Son of God? What mystery is committed to our stewardship and testimony, if not that?"

J.G. Bellett in 'The Son of God'.

1

INTRODUCTION

The construction of the ark

When the instructions for the building of the tabernacle were given, the first part of it as described in the Book of Exodus was, quite conspicuously, the ark of the covenant (Ex. 25:10-22). The description of God's dwelling place did not start from the **outside**, the court or the boards and the curtains of the tabernacle, but from the **inside**. And it did not start from the holy place, but from the Most Holy Place, the most sacred part of the tabernacle. Nobody was permitted to enter it, except Moses and the high priest – the latter once a year only and not without the blood of atonement. Here, in the Holiest of All, was the ark, the throne of God. And God started with the description of this vitally important part of the tabernacle when He revealed His plans about His dwelling place here on earth. The ark was built of the following parts:

The substructure
(1) a two and a half cubits long, a cubit and a half wide and a cubit and a half high chest of acacia wood,
(2) an overlay of pure gold, inside and outside,
(3) a moulding of gold around the ark on its upper side,
(4) four rings of gold, fastened on the four corners or possibly on the four feet of the ark,
(5) in the rings two poles, also of acacia wood and overlaid with gold;

The superstructure

(6) on top of the ark the mercy seat of pure gold, two and a half cubits long and a cubit and a half wide, probably resting within the above-mentioned moulding,

(7) at the two ends of the mercy seat two cherubim, made of one piece with the mercy seat and rising out of it, as it were. They faced one another, their wings covered the mercy seat and their faces were also turned toward the mercy seat.

This, roughly, is the description of the ark as we find it in Exodus 25 and 37. In Exodus 37 the construction of the ark comes **after** the building of the tabernacle and understandably so, because the construction of the tabernacle is seen here from the point of view of the responsibility of the people. In Exodus 25, however, we have God's side of the matter. When God describes His dwelling place, He **begins** with His throne. But from the point of view of man's responsibility it is impossible to build a throne for God without having built a dwelling place for Him first.

The ark did not just serve as God's throne, the place where Moses came to meet God and to receive His instructions, but also as a depository of the Testimony, that is, the law of the ten commandments: "And you shall put into the ark the Testimony which I will give you" (Ex. 25:16). To the people of Israel the law bore witness concerning God's rights and statutes: it was a letter to be read and kept by everybody. But since the people of Israel were not able to meet God's holy and just requirements – and neither was anybody else – the law was put into the ark. Here it was hidden from the eyes of man and what is more, covered by the blood-sprinkled mercy seat.

This revealed the need for atonement (cf. also Lev. 16). It pointed to the fact that only a substitutionary sacrifice could meet the requirements of the law. This is confirmed by Deuteronomy 10, where we are clearly told that the construction of the ark took place **after** the worship of the golden calf. When the people of Israel showed themselves incapable of keeping the law and almost immediately fell into idolatry, God looked for a safe depository for the second pair of tablets of stone that Moses had to hew for himself. The first pair of tablets had been broken by Moses at the foot of the mountain: in so doing he gave expression to the fact that Israel had broken God's law (Ex. 32). No doubt they would sin again, in spite of the grace which God had shown because of Moses' intercession. God had no other choice but to hide the law from the eyes of a sinful people who were unable to keep it. Henceforth the tablets of stone had to be kept in the ark.

The question arises as to whether Moses himself made the ark (as it says in Deut. 10), or whether Bezaleel built it (as is indicated in Ex. 37). Perhaps both men cooperated in constructing the ark. Another possibility is that Deuteronomy 10 regards Moses as the maker of the ark because he had ordered the work, surveyed it and approved of it – just as an artisan can employ other people to make his masterpieces. The last possibility is that Moses first made a temporary ark for the tablets of the law and that later on he put them into the ark constructed by Bezaleel – after the completion of the tabernacle (cf. Ex. 40: 20, but also 1 Ki. 8:9).

Now before going further into the meaning of the ark let us list its various parts with their different functions once more:

(1) The ark itself: a safe depository of God's holy law that could not be displayed openly amidst a sinful people.

(2) The rings and the poles: a necessity for carrying the ark through the wilderness. God's throne accompanied His wandering people.

(3) The moulding with the mercy seat and the cherubim: the actual throne of God's glory and at the same time the place where atonement was made.

In addition to that we find in the Book of Numbers and particularly in the earlier historical Books that the ark also served as the sign of God's presence in the struggle with Israel's enemies. These struggles were the "wars of the LORD", and so He Himself led His people in the battle.

The ark - the throne of the LORD

So we conclude that the ark had several functions and the most important of these was its serving as the throne of the God of Israel. From between the cherubim He spoke with Moses, the lawgiver of the people, and made known His commandments. In this way God reigned over His people and revealed His holy will to them.

Further, as a depository of the law, the ark was a fundamental part of the throne of God: so too was the golden mercy seat. The ark enclosing the law can be regarded as the foundation of God's throne, the just basis of His administration. For the law contained God's rules of life for His people. But since a sinful people could not meet His just requirements, another basis was needed upon which He could show them His grace. Now this need was met by the mercy seat, which was sprinkled with blood every year to make atonement for the sins of the people. This was the basis upon which God could, time and again, show His grace to sinful man. In Psalm 89:14 Ethan sings in a strikingly beautiful way of these two elements of God's government, both His righteousness and His grace:

> "Righteousness and justice are
> the foundation of Your throne;
> Mercy and truth go before Your face".

So God's government in the midst of His people really had a twofold character: it was a combination of both law and grace. God's grace was needed in order to meet man's sinful condition. In this connection we should also look at Exodus 34:6-7, where God's goodness and mercy are mentioned first. Were it not for this mingling with grace the people, who at Mount Sinai had formally put themselves under the law, could not have survived and neither could God have continued to dwell in the midst of them.

Apart from the ark itself and the mercy seat, the cherubim too, were an integral part of God's throne. God dwelt "between" or perhaps better, "above" (NASB), or "upon" (NEB) the cherubim. Ezekiel's vision of the throne speaks in favour of the latter version, for he saw the cherubim as bearers of the throne (Ezek. 1 and 10). In 1 Chronicles 28:2, David called the ark "the footstool of our God". But it can be argued in favour of the first view that God is also often seen as the LORD of hosts who is surrounded by His mighty angels, the servants who fulfil His words. They are subject to God's authority and see to the execution of His government.

The trouble as to the correct translation arises because in some cases the Hebrew text leaves out the preposition so that translators may choose between the prepositions "between" or "above" (1 Sam. 4:4; Ps. 80:1; 99:1). However, other Scriptures expressly say that God spoke with Moses from above the mercy seat, from **between** the two cherubim which were on the ark (Ex. 25:22; Num. 7:89). In any case it is quite clear that the cherubim are linked with God's presence in a particular way – either as its companions, or as its bearers. In Hebrews 9:5 they are called "the cherubim of glory overshadowing the mercy seat". They were made of pure gold and in the types of the Old Testament this was symbolical of the glory of God.

It is also remarkable that the cherubim and the mercy seat formed a whole and that the faces of the cherubim were turned toward the mercy seat. God's government is a gracious one, for it is based on the work of redemption. The garden of Eden was guarded by cherubim with a flaming sword in order to prevent fallen man from re-entering it (Gen. 3:24). But the cherubim at the two ends of God's throne cannot prevent man from approaching Him, for they are facing the blood-sprinkled mercy seat. They would love to look into the divine secret of the salvation of man (cf. 1 Pet. 1:12).

The different names of the ark

The names of the ark as given in Scripture confirm that it was
the throne of the God of Israel. Apart from the definitions "the
ark", "an ark of wood" and "an ark of acacia wood", six other
expressions can be found:

1. The ark of the Testimony

This definition is used notably in the Book of Exodus because
of the giving of the law on Mount Sinai. In the ark the tablets of
the law were to be kept safe from danger. They testified against
the people, because they spoke about God's just demands and
the resulting obligations (Ex. 25:22; 26:33-34; 30:6, 26; 31:7;
39:35; 40:3, 5, 21; Num. 4:5; 7:89; Josh. 4:16).

2. The ark of the covenant

Since the tablets of the law formed the basis of the covenant
which God had established with His people, they were also
called the tablets of the covenant and were placed in the ark of
the covenant. This expression occurs in a wide range of variations:
- "ark of the covenant" (Josh. 3:6, 8, 14; 4:9; 6:6; Heb. 9:4);
- "ark of the covenant of the LORD" (Num. 10:33; 14:44; Deut.
  10:8; 31:9, 25; Josh. 3:17; 4:7,18; 6:8; 8:33; 1 Sam. 4:3, 5; 1 Ki.
  3:15; 6:19; 8:1, 6; 1 Chr. 15:25-29; 16:37; 17:1; 22:19; 28:2, 18;
  2 Chr. 5:2, 7; Jer. 3:16);
- "ark of the covenant of God" (Judg. 20:27; 1 Sam. 4:4; 2 Sam.
  15:24; 1 Chr. 16:6);
- "ark of the covenant of the LORD your God" (Deut. 31:26; Josh.
  3:3);
- "ark of the covenant of the Lord (Adonai) of all the earth"
  (Josh. 3:11);
- "ark of the covenant of the LORD of hosts (Yahweh Sabaoth),
  who dwells between the cherubim" (1 Sam. 4:4).
- "the ark, in which is the covenant of the LORD which He made
  with the children of Israel" (2 Chr. 6:11).

3. The ark of the LORD

This name indicates how closely the presence of Yahweh, the covenant God, is connected with the ark. Here again, several variations can be found:
- "ark of the LORD" (Josh. 4:11; 6:6, 7, 11, 12, 13; 7:6; 1 Sam. 4:6; 5:3, 4; 6:1-21; 7:1; 2 Sam. 6:9-17; 1 Ki. 8:4; 1 Chr. 15:3; 16:4; 2 Chr. 8:11);
- "ark of the LORD (Yahweh), the Lord (Adonai) of all the earth" (Josh. 3:13);
- "ark of the LORD your God" (Josh. 4:5);
- "ark of the Lord GOD (Adonai Yahweh)" (1 Ki. 2:26);
- "ark of the LORD God of Israel" (1 Chr. 15:12,14).

4. The ark of God

This is a more general name, which sees God (Elohim) in His sublimity, strength and power rather than in His character as the God of the covenant. Again, there is much variety:
- "ark of God" (1 Sam. 3:3; 4:11-22; 5:1, 2, 10; 14:18; 2 Sam. 6: 3-12; 7:2;15:24, 25, 29; 1 Chr. 13:5, 7, 12, 14; 15:1, 2, 15, 24; 16:1; 2 Chr. 1:4);
- "ark of the God of Israel" (1 Sam. 5:7, 8, 10, 11; 6:3);
- "ark of our God" (1 Chr. 13:3);
- "ark of God, whose name is called by the Name, the LORD of Hosts, who dwells *between* the cherubim" (2 Sam. 6:2).
- "ark of God the LORD, who dwells *between* the cherubim, where *His* name is proclaimed" (1 Chr. 13:6). These last names are quite lengthy: the ark is the throne of God and the place with which His Name, that is, His Person and the divine presence are linked.

5. The ark of Your strength

This expression is used only twice, in Solomon's prayer during the consecratory ceremony of the temple and in Psalm 132 (cf. 2 Chr. 6:41; Ps. 132:8). The ark was the symbol of God's might that made the waters of the Jordan stand still and Israel's enemies tremble with fear.

6. The holy ark

We find this description but once. It is used by king Josiah at the celebration of the Passover (2 Chr. 35:3). Josiah was a great reformer who brought the people back to the worship of the LORD. In the same verse mention is also made of Levites who were "holy" to the LORD, i.e., dedicated to serving Him and especially set apart for that purpose. Of all the objects of the tabernacle the ark was the holiest part and as a consequence, it was placed in the Holiest of All.

The transportation of the ark

As we have seen already, the ark was the throne of Israel's God, the God of the covenant. It was erected in the sanctuary in the midst of God's people. But..... the Israelites were a pilgrim people, on their way through the wilderness to the Promised Land. And during all of the long journey from Egypt to Canaan God journeyed with them. The shining cloud of His presence itself, which covered the tabernacle, went before them and showed them which way they had to go. But for this reason the sanctuary and the ark too, had to be transportable. That was the purpose of the poles on either side of the ark; they had to remain in the rings of the ark and were not to be taken from it (Ex. 25:15).

Perhaps they were partially removed and drawn out so that they were visible from the holy place after the ark had reached its final resting place in the temple (1 Ki. 8:8; 2 Chr. 5:9). The Hebrew wording in these verses is obscure and therefore, others translate that the poles were so long that the ends were visible from the holy place before the inner sanctuary (NIV, NASB).

But there was one more provision for the transportation of the ark: before the Levites came to carry it, the priests had to cover it with several coverings and insert the poles. The same thing was done with the other holy vessels of the tabernacle:

the table of showbread, the lampstand, the golden altar, the bronze altar of burnt offering and all the necessary utensils (Num. 4:1-15). Only the laver is not mentioned, which may imply that it was transported without any covering. All the holy vessels were covered with two coverings, except the ark of the Testimony and the table of showbread. For them no less than three coverings were used.

The coverings of the ark were:

(1) The veil that separated the holy place from the Most Holy.

(2) A covering of badger skins – or seals' skins (JND), or hides of sea cows (NIV), or porpoise skins (NASB, NEB) –, a species of leather that was also used for the outside covering of the tabernacle.

(3) A cloth entirely of blue, or "pure blue" (NASB).

The order of the coverings is interesting, because in all other cases the last one was always a covering of badger skins – very probably because it was weather-proof. Thus, when the ark was carried through the wilderness, it stood out from the other holy articles by its unique blue covering. Everybody could see this was the holiest part of the tabernacle: the throne of glory of the LORD. Blue is the colour of heaven.

It was the task of the priests to prepare everything that had to be transported, but for the carrying itself the Levites were responsible, namely the family of the Kohathites – the next of kin of the priests. This was so because of the absolute holiness of these vessels: only the priests were allowed to cover them with the various coverings, to remove the poles and to insert them again. It was only after these preparations had been made that the Levites were permitted to enter the sanctuary and shoulder the poles. They were not allowed to see or touch the holy things themselves, so that they would not die (cf. Num. 4: 15ff.; 18:2-3; 2 Sam. 6:6-7).

While the other families of the Levites had carts to transport the boards, the pillars and the coverings of the tabernacle

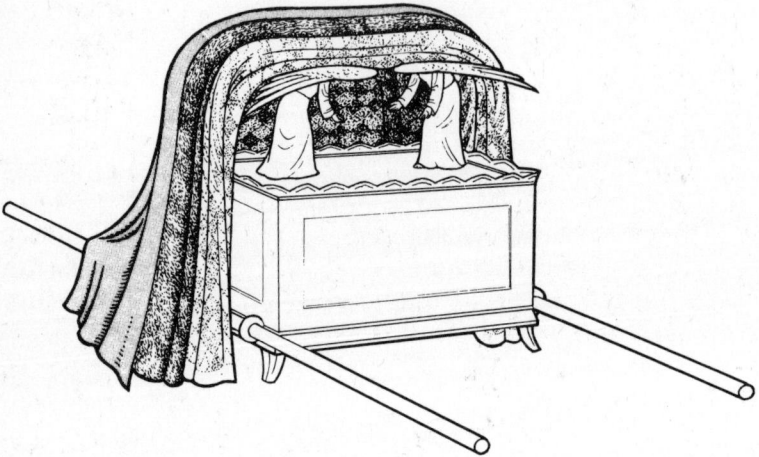

Careful attention had to be given to the transportation of the ark. The ark is a type of Christ, and the testimony concerning our Lord has been entrusted now to His people while they are on their way to a heavenly country. In the same way as the ark journeyed with Israel, Christ desires to go with us.

and so on, the Kohathites had not. They had to carry the holy objects on their shoulders alone (Num. 7:6-9; 1 Chr. 15:15; 2 Chr. 35:3). In fact, David made a grave mistake when he tried to bring the ark to Jerusalem on a new cart (see 1 Chr. 13 and 15). It had to be reverently carried on the shoulders of the Levites.

On other solemn occasions, however, the priests also are mentioned as bearers of the ark: at the crossing of the Jordan, during the conquest of Jericho, at the renewal of the covenant at Mount Ebal (Josh. 3, 6 and 8 resp.) and also at the dedication of the temple of Solomon (1 Ki. 8). But these are exceptions to the general rule. We must bear in mind that the priests bore the final responsibility of the service of the tabernacle and that the Levites were appointed to help them in that service (Num. 3 and 8).

We have dealt with this subject – the transportation of the ark – in some detail, because it is important to our whole study of the journey of the ark from Mount Sinai to its final resting place on Mount Moriah. But before we can proceed with that we must first study the typical meaning of the ark itself and the meaning of its transportation.

The ark - a type of Christ

God's dwelling place
The tabernacle and all that was in it were copies and shadows of the heavenly things (Heb. 8:5; 9:23). The tabernacle was the dwelling place of God and, consequently, it first of all spoke of heaven itself, where God sits enthroned. He dwells in a high and holy place; He looks down from heaven and from His holy habitation; heaven is His throne (Isa. 57:15; 63:15; 66:1). Just as on the Day of Atonement the high priest entered the Most Holy Place, Christ has now entered into heaven itself (Heb. 9:24). On this line of thought the court of the tabernacle symbolizes a holy place on earth where the people of God gather to meet their God, the holy place itself typifies the heavenly places

or realms (Eph. 1:3) and the Holiest, "the heaven of heavens" (1 Ki. 8:27), or "the third heaven" (2 Cor. 12:2).

But from another point of view Christ Himself is God's dwelling place. It pleased the Father that all the fullness of the Godhead should dwell in Him (Col. 1:19; 2:9). Therefore, Christ could compare the temple of Jerusalem to "the temple of His body" (John 2:19-21). God dwelt in Christ bodily and revealed Himself to mankind; and whoever came to Christ could approach God through Him. Accordingly, the New Testament makes it perfectly clear that the various parts of God's dwelling place in the Old Testament were typical of Christ. Thus the veil in the holy place speaks of the flesh of Christ, His human body (Heb. 10:20). And in Romans 3 we read about His atoning death, by which He became the true mercy seat or throne of grace: "Christ Jesus, whom God set forth *to be* a propitiation by His blood" (v. 25). The literal translation of the word "propitiation" is "mercy seat"; we find the same Greek word in Hebrews 9:5.

These latter Scriptures bring us nearer to the heart of our subject, namely that we are to look at the ark as a type of Christ. It may be noted in passing, however, that in the present time there is even a third divine dwelling place: the Church of the living God, which is a habitation of God in the Spirit (Eph. 2:20-22; 1 Tim. 3:15; Heb. 3:6). And in this house of God, "the ark", that is Christ Himself, occupies a central place. In Christ, God dwells in the midst of His own. We are under the gracious rule of the Son of His love, who accomplished the work of redemption for us (Col. 1:13,14).

Acacia wood and pure gold

But let us now turn to the typical meaning of the ark itself. This throne of God consisted of two different materials: it was made of wood and of gold. In the Septuagint, the shittim or acacia wood is rendered by the term "incorruptible wood". This wood speaks to us of the unique humanity of Christ, who as a Rod came forth from the stem of Jesse, as a root out of dry ground (Isa. 11:1; 53:2). God would not allow His Son, His Holy One, to see corruption (Ps. 16:10,11; Acts 2:22ff.).

The precious pure gold with which the wood was overlaid speaks of the divine glory of His Person. As these two materials were united in the ark, Christ is God and man in one Person. God dwells in Him bodily, and today He is still present in the midst of His own by His Spirit.

The tablets of stone

In the ark the two stone tablets were kept. But Christ had the law written in His heart. He said, "I delight to do Your will, O my God, and Your law *is* within my heart" (Ps. 40:8). It was His food to do the will of Him who sent Him and to finish His work (John 4:34). Now that divine will went much further than the law required. For the law did *not* require that a Just should die for the unjust. And yet Christ sacrificed His holy and pure life to glorify God and to redeem sinners. That is why Psalm 40 links the fulfilling of the will of God with this perfect sacrifice (cf. Ps. 40:6-8 with Heb. 10:5-10).

The mercy seat

The ark was the base on which the mercy seat rested, and in the same way Christ's perfect life was the basis of His sacrifice. The ark and the blood-sprinkled mercy seat could not be seen separate and in the same way Christ's work of redemption cannot be separated from His unique Person. It was He – both God and man and yet one Christ – who has given Himself for us, an offering and a sacrifice to God.

Maybe the fact that the mercy seat was made of pure gold would show us that Christ accomplished the work of redemption in the power of His deity. No man could give satisfaction on behalf of man. Christ alone was able to pay the ransom, because He was both man and God.

The cherubim

The mercy seat and the cherubim that rose from it at either end made up the actual throne of God. In Hebrews 9:5 the cherubim are called "the cherubim of glory". They speak of the divine authority that has been given to Christ, which is now being exercised by Him for the sake of His gracious government. All glory belongs to Him. He who died is the risen and glorified Lord. He has all authority both in heaven and on earth. It is a wonderful assurance to know that His divine authority is based on His accomplished work of redemption – just as the cherubim *rested* on the mercy seat.

The throne of grace

For that reason God's throne in the midst of His people is a throne of grace and His rule is a gracious one. In Christ, God dwells amongst His redeemed people and His reign in their midst is conditioned by His grace. Just as the ark was the central point of the people of Israel and the tribes camping around it – first the tribe of Levi, the priests and the Levites, then the other tribes – so our Lord Jesus Christ now is the true Centre of His own. They are gathered together in His name, and there He is in their midst (Matt. 18:20).

But this also means that Christ has all authority in the midst of His own and that He is recognized by them as such. If things are all right, decisions taken in the Church of God are decisions of Christ Himself, decisions "from His throne". In the same way as God communicated to His earthly people His laws from the ark (His throne on earth), through Christ He has manifested His will to His heavenly people. Every believer ought to recognize this revealed will when reading the Word of God. Are we personally and collectively subject to this divine authority in our midst?

Christ our Centre and our Companion

It is important that the people of Israel were a pilgrim people. This meant that the sanctuary – including the ark – had to be transported in their midst during the long journey through the wilderness. Their destination was the land of Canaan and there the ark would find a permanent resting place. The lesson for us is quite clear. As Christians we journey through this world towards our heavenly destination – for here we have no continuing city, but we seek the one to come. And on this pilgrimage we carry with us the testimony concerning the Lord Jesus Christ, just like the people of Israel carried the ark during their wanderings in the wilderness. So, when we speak about the ark being carried by God's people, the question arises, "Do we, so to speak, carry Him around, do we honour His name appropriately during our walk here on earth?"

Christ is not only the One who is our Centre when we gather together in His name as God's people, He also accompanies us on all the steps of our pathway. He is our faithful Companion in all our experiences in the wilderness, in all the trials and testings that fall to the lot of God's people in this world. Do we realize this and do we treat Him with due reverence? Are we conscious of the presence of God Himself, in the Person of Christ and in the Holy Spirit, in our midst? (cf. 1 Cor. 14:25).

That is why the story of the ark of God is so important to us. In it we find many lessons as to how we should handle the precious testimony concerning the Person of Christ, which has been entrusted to us. No doubt the reverence with which the priests and the Levites treated the ark has much to tell us. Of this we shall say more when we discuss the different coverings of the ark in the next chapter.

2

FROM MOUNT SINAI TO SHILOH (1)

At the mountain of God

When God had redeemed His people from bondage in Egypt, He bore them on eagles' wings and brought them **to Himself** (Ex. 19:4). He brought them out of the land of Egypt. He led them straight through the Red Sea and on through the wilderness to Mount Sinai. There He would reveal Himself to the people which He had delivered and set apart from all the peoples of the earth to be His own possession, His own special people. The Israelites were to be to Him "a kingdom of priests and a holy nation" (Ex. 19:6).

So here we see a people delivered from the enemy who had had them at his mercy. Henceforth they would be entirely dedicated to their God. They were in God's presence, camping around the mountain where He dwelt and where He spoke to the people of His possession in order to make His mind known to them. It was God's desire to dwell in their midst for ever. But this could be realized only when a dwelling place had been prepared for Him!

Now this is the grand theme of the second part of the Book of Exodus: the construction of the tabernacle, a tent dwelling for the LORD their God. Moses had to order the Israelites to build this sanctuary in accordance with the pattern shown to him on the mountain by God Himself. The divine command was: "And let them make Me a sanctuary, that I may dwell among them. According to all that I show you, *that is*, the pattern of the tabernacle and the pattern of all its furnishings, just so you shall make it" (Ex. 25:8-9; cf. v. 40 and Heb. 8:5).

These words in Exodus 25 are immediately followed by the description of the ark of the Testimony, God's throne in the midst of His people. This was the place where Moses had to approach God to receive His commandments: "And there I will meet with you; and I will speak with you from above the mercy seat, from between the two cherubim which *are* on the ark of the Testimony, of all *things* which I will give you in commandment to the children of Israel" (v. 22).

In the next chapter we read in which part of the tabernacle the ark had to be placed: not in the first part, the holy place, but behind the veil in the Holiest of All (Ex. 26:33-34). Thus there was nothing else in the Most Holy Place than the throne of the LORD. The veil separated it from the other holy vessels in the sanctuary. Here, only Moses was allowed to enter freely. And the high priest could do so once a year when he approached the throne with the blood of atonement to sprinkle it on and in front of the mercy seat.

Exodus 30 gives some details about the location of the ark and its consecration with the holy anointing oil. Its position should be in line with the altar of incense, which stood on the other side of the veil in the holy place (v. 6). When the tabernacle was anointed the ark, too, had to be sanctified with the holy anointing oil (v. 26). Then, in Exodus 31, two exceedingly gifted men are appointed to carry out the work. The names of these two men – Bezaleel and Aholiab – mean "in God's shadow, or protection", and "tent of the father" respectively. These beautiful names reflected the task they had to accomplish, the construction of God's dwelling place.

Then the narrative is interrupted by the sad story of the golden calf (Ex. 32-34). Only because of Moses' intercession could mercy be shown to the sinning people, who were so quick to turn their backs on their God. From Exodus 35 on we find a detailed description of the construction work of the tabernacle that was carried out by Bezaleel and Aholiab and their fellow workers. Everything was done in accordance with the instructions previously given by God to Moses in Exodus 25 through 30.

The Book of Exodus ends with Moses' approval of the whole work and his personal involvement in setting up the tabernacle (Ex. 39 and 40). The ark which Bezaleel had made (Ex. 37:1-9), was also brought to Moses for inspection and thereupon it was given its place in the tabernacle. When the tabernacle was erected, Moses acted as follows: "He took the Testimony and put *it* into the ark, inserted the poles through the rings of the ark, and put the mercy seat on top of the ark. And he brought the ark into the tabernacle, hung up the veil of the covering, and partitioned off the ark of the Testimony, as the LORD had commanded Moses" (Ex. 40:20-21).

Exactly one year after the exodus from Egypt Moses set up the tabernacle (Ex. 40:2, 17). And the crowning glory of his work was the moment when the LORD Himself took up His residence in the tent dwelling. When Moses had finished the work, it says: "Then the cloud covered the tabernacle of meeting, and the glory of the LORD filled the tabernacle" (Ex. 40:34). From now on, the pillar of cloud and the pillar of fire that went before the people during their exodus from Egypt (Ex. 13:21-22), and which rested on Mount Sinai when the law was given there (24:15-17), rested on the tabernacle. God had made His abode in His sanctuary. The bright cloud of His presence had found a resting place in the midst of His people and it would go with them throughout all their journeys (Ex. 40:36-38).

The Church as a spiritual house

The house built by Moses as a servant of God, was the Old Testament type of the spiritual house built by Christ as the Son of God (Heb. 3:1-6). The tabernacle was the copy and shadow of the better and heavenly things that came in when Christ came down here and when the Holy Spirit descended afterwards. The end of the Book of Exodus has its New Testament counterpart in the beginning of the Book of Acts. Just as the cloud covered the tent of meeting and the glory of the LORD filled the tabernacle (Ex. 40), the Spirit of God filled the Church which Christ had built by virtue of His death and resurrection (Acts 2). Moses was the builder of an earthly, material sanctuary, but Christ is the Builder of a heavenly and spiritual house, a lasting and imperishable dwelling place.

Just like Moses led God's people out of the land of Egypt, our Lord Jesus Christ delivered His people from this present evil age (Gal. 1:4). Moses delivered Israel from the power of Pharaoh, but Christ delivered His own from the power of the ruler of this world, that is, Satan (John 16:11,33). The Red Sea once for all separated the Israelites from the land where they used to live in slavery. Similarly, by the death of Christ we have been delivered for ever from the bondage of sin and from Satan's power (Rom. 6-8). We now belong to the risen Lord and we are under His authority, in the same way as the Israelites, when departing from Egypt, put themselves under the authority of Moses (cf. 1 Cor. 10:1-2).

Moses led the people of Israel to the mountain **of God** (that is what Mount Sinai is called in Ex. 3:1; 18:5; 24:13). This means that he brought the people into God's presence and it was God's intention to dwell for ever in the midst of His redeemed. In the same way Christ, the Author of our salvation, has brought us **to God** (cf. 1 Pet. 3:18). It is God's intention that we, as His redeemed, should dwell in His presence and should listen to His Word. As grateful children of God, as a family of kings and priests we surround our God and pay homage to Him because of the great things He has done for us.

In the same way as the glory of the Lord filled the tabernacle built by Moses and the Israelites, the indwelling Spirit now fills the Church. The family of the redeemed is at the same time the spiritual house in which God dwells. God's household constitutes also His house, His habitation. We find this twofold meaning of the word "house" several times in Scripture (cf. 2 Sam. 7). On the day of Pentecost, the Holy Spirit filled the spiritual house of God. For we read in Acts 2: "And it **filled** the whole house where they were sitting...And they were all **filled** with the Holy Spirit" (vv. 2,4). According to the promise of our Lord the Holy Spirit will dwell for ever in the Church. The Spirit of truth abides with us for ever. He dwells with us and will be in us (John 14:16-17).

One aspect of the tabernacle as a type is that it clearly faces us with our responsibility as believers. Moses and the Israelites together constructed God's dwelling place and for that purpose they brought voluntary offerings (Ex. 25 and 35). When God by His Spirit has made His abode in us and dwells in our midst, we are all involved in the practical realization of this great blessing. The believers who had gathered together on the day of Pentecost were longing for the Comforter to come, who would endue them with power from on high. They were prepared to be filled with the Spirit and from that moment on, they put themselves wholly under His guidance.

Of course, we cannot impair the glorious presence of the Spirit here below, for this is based on the finished work of Christ and His glorification in heaven alone. But when it comes to our being a "habitation of God" in a practical way, our real spiritual condition is of the greatest importance. God only dwells where He finds a resting place, where there are hearts prepared to give Him the place which is His due, where brethren really dwell together in unity (Ps. 133:1). We all are responsible for realizing in a practical way this tremendous privilege of being God's dwelling place. If we grieve or quench the Spirit (Eph. 4:30; 1 Thess. 5:19), we will not experience much of being a habitation of God in the Spirit. In that case God's presence might even have to leave us – just as later on in Israel's history the glory of the LORD had to be withdrawn from that people!

The journey through the wilderness

At the mountain of God Israel received God's laws. But it was not God's purpose for His people to stay there. He desired to bring them into the Promised Land and to give them an inheritance of their own. He journeyed with them in the sanctuary the Israelites had constructed for Him, so that He could always make known to Moses His will for them. Thus, after a number of preparations at Mount Sinai, the moment came for them to dismantle the camp and to continue their journey to the land of Canaan, with God's dwelling place in their midst.

The account of Israel's journey through the wilderness is found in the Book of Numbers. And here we come across numerous details about the transportation of the tabernacle and of the ark, God's throne, about the order in which the tribes of Israel had to march out and so on. To some of these particulars we now give our attention[1].

The central place of the tabernacle

When one reads the first chapters of Numbers, it is to be noted that the tabernacle occupied a central place in the midst of the tribes of Israel: "Then the tabernacle of meeting shall move out with the camp of the Levites in the middle of the camps; as they camp, so they shall move out, everyone in his place, by their standards" (Num. 2:17). The tribe of Levi camped next to the dwelling place of God, surrounding it, because the priests and the Levites were responsible for attending to the duties of the sanctuary. The other tribes camped around it in a wider circle. As we have already noted, this shows the central place Christ occupies amongst His people who are gathered together in His name (Matt. 18:20).

It appears from Numbers 2:17 that the divine order had also to be maintained when the camp was taken down. The sanctuary still retained its central place in the long tribal train. According to Numbers 10 the correct order for the people to set out in, was:

(1) the pillar of cloud;

(2) the three tribes on the east side (Judah, Issachar, Zebu-lun);

(3) the sons of Gershon and the sons of Merari, who transported the coverings, the hangings, the pillars and the boards of the tabernacle on carts;

(4) the three tribes on the south side (Reuben, Simeon, Gad);

(5) the Kohathites, carrying the most holy things: the ark of the Testimony, the altar of incense, the table of showbread, the lampstand, the laver and the altar of burnt offering;

(6) the three tribes on the west side (Ephraim, Manasseh, Benjamin);

(7) the three tribes on the north side (Dan, Asher, Naphtali).

Thus the holy vessels of the tabernacle were exactly in the middle of the train, both preceded and followed by six tribes. The structure itself was taken down earlier and it was carried before the holy things, so that it could be set up and prepared before the Kohathites arrived with their precious burden (Num. 10:21). These objects speak of the Person of Christ in a very special way. If we apply these things to ourselves, it suggests that Christ is not only in our midst in our resting places in the wilderness, but also all along the pathway which we, as pilgrims, have to go. When we are "camping" around Him, He is in our midst. But He is also with us every day of our marching on from one oasis to another. Christ is **leading** us by His Spirit. This is indicated by the type of the pillar of cloud, which went **before** the Israelites and showed them the way. But the Lord is also **in our midst** as we travel along, as is indicated by the central place of the ark in the tribal train. Christ is the centre of our testimony here below, for we carry the testimony concerning His precious Person with us and are presenting Him to the outside world.

The coverings of the ark

But this should be done with due reverence and prudence. This is the typical meaning of the various coverings with which the priests had to cover the ark before the Levites could carry it. The ark had to be treated with great care, as also, indeed, the other holy things. According to Numbers 4 three coverings were needed for the ark. First of all the veil, which separated the Holiest from the holy place. In Numbers 4:5 it is called "the covering veil" and in Exodus 40:21 "the veil of the covering", so as to partition off the ark and hide it from the eyes of the priests serving in the holy place. Another expression, "the veil of the Testimony", is found in Leviticus 24:3. This refers to its hiding both the ark and its contents, the two tablets of the Testimony.

So all these Scriptures closely link the veil with the ark. The veil hid the throne of God from the eyes of man: it did so when the tabernacle had been set up, and it did so when it was being transported through the wilderness. The veil woven of blue, purple, scarlet and fine linen thread, with an artistic design of cherubim, which itself was one of the most beautiful parts of the tabernacle, served as a covering for the most holy vessel, the ark. There God sat enthroned: with the ark He had linked His presence.

Hebrews 10:20 tells us that the veil is a type of Christ's flesh, that is, of Christ's life here on earth. When He died, the veil in the temple was torn in two from top to bottom. Because of the death of Christ, God Himself opened up access to His throne. Christ's perfect life could not bring us to God. To accomplish that it was necessary that His life should be cut off and that He should die. Nevertheless, the life of our Lord Jesus Christ occupies a very important place in our testimony here on earth. We must often repeat that He was and still is the perfectly righteous One (this is shown in type by the fine linen thread of the veil), the Man from heaven (the blue), the Son of man, whose reign is universal (the purple), and the King of Israel (the scarlet). And also that all authority has been given to Him (the cherubim).

Both the veil and the ark are types of Christ. When we carry "the ark" with us, in other words, when we carry the testimony with us concerning the great truths of God's revelation in the Person of Christ and His redemptive work (on the basis of which God now dwells in our midst), we can never dissociate this from Christ's unique manhood and His personal glories as shown in type in the veil.

When the ark was carried, it had to be covered with a second covering, of badger skins and finally with a third cloth entirely of blue (Num. 4:6). Badger skins were weatherproof. For that reason the outer covering of the tabernacle itself was made of the same material. This indicates that we should guard our testimony concerning Christ against all sorts of harmful influences from outside, against every "wind of doctrine", trying to derogate from His Person (Eph. 4:14). But the outer covering of the ark was a cloth entirely of blue, thereby distinguishing the ark from all the other holy vessels of the tabernacle – all of which had an outer covering of badger skins. Thus, the ark, being the most important part of the tent dwelling, was clearly discernible. The Levites who carried the ark on their shoulders, paying personal reverence to it, were thoroughly aware of the importance of their duty. And likewise, in our testimony concerning the Person of Christ we should stress the fact that He was a unique **heavenly** Person, the One in whom the Father was well pleased.

The ark went before them

Finally, we should mention that when the children of Israel set out from Mount Sinai, not only the pillar of cloud, but also the ark went ahead of them to seek out a resting place for the people of God (see Num. 10:29-36). This exceptional position of the ark must be explained in the light of the request that Moses made to his brother-in-law Hobab, to go with them and show them the way through the wilderness. This request revealed a lack of confidence in God's guidance. It was not Hobab who would be their eyes (v. 31), but God Himself who would be their Guide to the Promised Land. Therefore, when they left the mountain of God, the ark, with which God had linked His presence, took the lead (v. 33).

In this connection the last two verses of Numbers 10 are important too, since they show the great reverence with which Moses treated the ark. Whenever the ark set out, Moses said: "Rise up, O LORD! Let Your enemies be scattered, and let those who hate You flee before You". And when it rested, he said: "Return, O LORD, *to* the many thousands of Israel". Moses spoke these words fully aware that the ark represented God Himself: "Rise up, O LORD!", and: "Return, O LORD". God Himself went ahead of His people, scattering their enemies, and then returned in blessing to the many thousands of Israel.

Israel's failure in the wilderness

As we have already noted, the Book of Numbers contains the account of Israel's journey through the wilderness to the land of God's promise. In the first ten chapters the preparations for the journey are described, but the second part of the Book shows us how Israel failed during these wilderness years (Num. 11-25).

Numbers 14
It was one sad chorus, an account of grumbling and complaining, culminating in the unbelieving people's refusal to take possession of the Promised Land. When this occurred, the LORD said: "They have put Me to the test now these **ten** times, and have not heeded My voice" (Num. 14:22).

In this context our attention is drawn to the final verses of Numbers 14, because here again, the ark of the covenant is mentioned. Here the ark did not go victoriously at the head of the people, but it remained in the camp (vv. 39-45). God could not go with His people when they refused to repent of their unbelief. He had said that they would have to wander in the wilderness for forty years (vv. 33-34). But yet, instead of submitting themselves to this sentence, the Israelites attempted to go up to the land of Canaan. Their claim to be acting in accordance with God's promises, however, was a transgression of the clear command of the Lord. He could not now go with them to drive out the enemy from before them. It is striking, indeed, to read in verse 44 after Moses' warning: "But they presumed to go up to the mountaintop; nevertheless, neither the ark of the covenant of the LORD nor Moses departed from the camp".

At this juncture Moses showed himself to be truly subject to God's word and to have a right understanding of His mind. If God be for us, who shall be against us? No enemy will then be able to withstand us. But if God is against us and cannot approve our human plans and thoughts, who shall be for us? Then we cannot but succumb to the power of the enemy – just as Israel did here. What we are taught here is that we cannot do anything without God. As the Lord told His disciples: "...for without Me you can do nothing" (John 15:5).

Numbers 16

In Numbers 16 we come to the second climax of Israel's failure in the wilderness: the rebellion of Korah, Dathan and Abiram. They disputed the leadership of Moses and Aaron, and particularly the God-ordained priesthood of Aaron (see Num. 16:3-11,40). Having judged the insurgents, God confirmed the Aaronic priesthood by an extra sign: the blossoming rod of Aaron. In one night it had sprouted and put forth buds, had produced blossoms and yielded ripe almonds. Therefore, this rod – the symbol of Aaron's authority and dignity – had to be brought back before the Testimony. It should be kept before the ark containing the two tablets of the Testimony as a sign against the rebels (Num. 17:10).

In Hebrews 9:4, we are even told that Aaron's rod that budded was kept **in** the ark of the covenant, together with the

golden pot that had the manna (cf. Ex. 16:33-34) and the tablets
of the covenant. The exact location of this rod and the golden
pot containing the manna is something of a problem, though,
because at the dedication of the temple it is explicitly stated
that there was "nothing in the ark except the two tablets of
stone which Moses put there at Horeb" (1 Ki. 8:9; 2 Chr. 5:10).
The explanation could be that the rod of Aaron and the pot that
had the manna were in the ark for some time, but were
removed later. This would agree with the Scriptures already
referred to (Ex. 16:33-34 and Num. 17:10), where it says that
these objects should be put **before** the Testimony and be kept
there.

   The typical teaching is no problem for us, because all these
objects speak about the Person of Christ Himself. The pot that
had the manna speaks of Him as the bread which came down
from heaven (cf. John 6). The remembrance of this bread from
heaven, the true Bread of life, will be kept for ever (cf. Ex. 16:
32). Its value is eternal, even when our pilgrim life has ended.
The manna was Israel's food in the desert only. It ceased after
they had eaten the produce of the land of Canaan (Josh. 5:12).

   In contrast with the manna (which speaks of Christ's life on
earth), the blossoming rod of Aaron points to Christ's resurrection and its wonderful results. In the manna we see Christ
as He came down into our circumstances here on earth, serving
as our spiritual food. But in the blossoming rod of Aaron we see
the power of His resurrection-life. Christ has become a priest
for ever "according to the power of an endless – or, indestructi-
ble – life" (Heb. 7:16-17). The almond is the first fruit tree that
blossoms; when it does so it is still winter. It is a symbol of
the budding new life, and forebodes the end of the wintertime.
In Hebrew, the words for "to be awake" and "almond" are
identical (cf. Jer. 1:11-12). As the risen One, Christ is now a
priest for ever in the heavenly sanctuary. By His death and
resurrection He bore much fruit, and raised us to life with Him.
He now carries us in the presence of God as the One who made
it perfectly clear that **only** He could bring forth life in the midst

of death – precisely as **only** the rod of the priest chosen by God could yield ripe almonds (Num. 17).

What a privilege it is for us to know Christ in this way in the various aspects of His Person! We have already referred to the ark itself and the two tablets of the law as being typical of Christ as the One who perfectly fulfilled the will of God and made atonement for His people. The ark with the mercy seat shows us the mystery of His Person as both God and man, and His atoning death. The pot containing the manna reminds us of the fact that He is the living bread which came down from heaven. The blossoming rod of Aaron is a type of Him as the risen One, who has received an eternal and unchangeable priesthood.

It is in this way we may know Him on our journey through the wilderness, on our pilgrimage here below. In this way we also have to learn to know Him when even those who confess His name rise up against His authority as the Apostle and High Priest of our confession (Heb. 3:1). For the uprising of Korah, Dathan and Abiram typifies the rejection of the apostleship and the priesthood of Christ by nominal Christians. All too often, the authority of God's Word has been attacked or even replaced by the authority of human traditions, and the unique priesthood of Christ has been put aside by a human priesthood imagining it could mediate between God and men. In this situation of breakdown we need to put ourselves under the authority of Christ as the true Moses and the true Aaron. Only His Word has absolute authority and only His priesthood is recognized by God and is able to grant us new life.

Numbers 31

The next incident during the wilderness journey in which the ark played a part can be found in Numbers 31. This chapter belongs to the third main part of the Book (Num. 26-36), which was written with a view to the entry into the Promised Land. After Balaam had blessed God's people, he taught Balak to put a stumbling block before the children of Israel by tempting them to eat things sacrificed to idols and to commit sexual immorality (Num. 25; 31:16; cf. Rev. 2:14). After the Israelites had mixed with the Moabites there would be no need for Balak to fear them any longer.

This ruse did succeed, but not entirely, thanks to the resolute action of Phinehas, Aaron's grandson. In Numbers 31 he was put in charge of an expedition against the Midianites. In verse 6, we read that Phinehas was sent to the war "with the holy articles (or, instruments) and the signal trumpets in his hand". This expression, "the holy articles", often refers to all the things needed for the service of the tabernacle, but it is also used of the holy vessels themselves (the ark, the golden altar, the lampstand, etc.). So probably the ark went with them on this expedition, just as it did on other occasions when Israel went to war. Moreover, the trumpets that are mentioned here are found more often in combination with the ark (cf. Num. 10; Josh. 6; 1 Chr. 15:24; 16:6). The priests were to blow them before the ark of God. And because God went with them, Phinehas won a complete victory over the enemy.

Now what is the message of this story for us? In the course of its history the professing Church too, has mixed with the world and the result has been spiritual fornication with the world powers (cf. Rev. 2:14 as well as Rev. 17 and 18). This evil can only be combatted if Christ Himself goes with us and if we give heed to the trumpet of His Word.

Consequently, all the incidents in the Book of Numbers[2] in which the ark figures teach us importants lessons. If God goes with us, we can go to war. If He stays in the camp, we should remain quietly waiting in His presence. Without the ark Israel could neither advance through the wilderness, nor take possession of the Promised Land. Without Christ we are no match for the wiles of the devil, for on our own we are incapable of walking to His honour and of taking possession of our heavenly inheritance. This can be done only at His time and in His way, as we now hope to see in the Book of Joshua.

Notes

1. It may be noted in passing, however, that in the preceding Book of Leviticus the ark is mentioned but once, namely in the central chapter 16, which describes the ritual of the Day of Atonement. After the death of the two sons of Aaron, the high priest, when they offered profane fire before the LORD, Aaron's entry into the Most Holy Place was restricted to once a year only on this annual occasion (Lev. 10:1-2; 16:1-2). In contrast to this, the Christian can approach the throne of grace at all times through the veil (Heb. 4:16; 10:19-22).

2. In Deuteronomy the ark is mentioned several times, but it is not necessary for us to deal with these passages in detail. We referred to Deuteronomy 10 when speaking about the construction of the ark. It is mentioned further only in chapter 31, where we see that the book of the law of Moses was put beside the ark of the covenant, that it might be there as a witness against Israel (v. 26). Likewise, the Lord is observing us to see whether we obey His Word or not.

3

FROM MOUNT SINAI TO SHILOH (2)

Israel crosses the Jordan

After the journey through the wilderness we now come to the second stage of the ark's journey: its entry into the land of Canaan. There it was placed in the sanctuary at Shiloh, the first permanent resting place of the ark in the Promised Land. Before the people could enter the land, however, they were faced with a tremendous obstacle. The river Jordan blocked the entry into the land, and as Joshua 3:15 tells us, at that time the Jordan overflowed all its banks. So there was a very great barrier between the people and the land that God had promised to give them. How could they bridge it?

There was but one answer to this problem: only **God** could clear the way for His people. He had divided the waters of the Red Sea, so that the children of Israel could cross it and in doing so they were for ever delivered from the land of slavery. And now again, He was about to show His might and clear a way through the waters of the Jordan in order to lead Israel into the Promised Land, a land flowing with milk and honey. How was He going to do this? *By means of the ark!*

When they had crossed the Red Sea the **staff** of Moses, the staff of judgment that had brought the plagues on Egypt, was used to divide the waters. But for the Jordan crossing the **ark** of God was used. When the feet of the carriers of the ark dipped in the edge of the water, the waters were cut off and the people of God crossed over on dry ground, past the ark being held in the river bed, and they set foot on the inheritance they had been

The waters of the Jordan were cut off before the ark of God's strength. The psalmist refers to this event as follows: "What ails you, O Jordan, that you turned back?...Tremble, O earth, at the presence of the Lord" (Ps. 114:5, 7). Christ went into death and triumphed over it. Since He cleared the way across the river of death, there is a safe passage for us too.

looking forward to for so many years.

Thus, when Israel crossed the Jordan, the ark was the central point. All eyes were turned towards it. When the ark set out the people set out from their place as well and went after it. The officers commanded the people, saying, "When you see the ark of the covenant of the LORD your God, and the priests, the Levites, bearing it, then you shall set out from your place and go after it. Yet there shall be a space between you and it, about two thousand cubits by measure. Do not come near it, that you may know the way by which you must go, for you have not passed this way before". And Joshua said to the people, "Sanctify yourselves, for tomorrow the LORD will do wonders among you" (Josh. 3:3-5).

The people then followed the ark along its route, though at a respectful distance. As soon as the feet of the priests who bore the ark touched the edge of the water, the waters were divided, so that a way was paved for the people of God. So they crossed over, filing past the ark being held in the midst of the Jordan, and profoundly aware of the fact that only by means of the ark the entrance into the land had been opened to them. It was the ark of the LORD (Yahweh), who remembered His covenant with His people. And He was at the same time "the Lord (Adonai) of all the earth", the rightful Owner of the land and of all the earth, who was now about to make His people take possession of their inheritance (Josh. 3:13).

Two memorials of twelve stones were set up: one of them in the midst of the Jordan, in the place where the priests who bore the ark stood, and the other in the camp at Gilgal. The memorial in Gilgal would be a sign to future generations "that the waters of the Jordan were cut off before the ark of the covenant of the LORD" (Josh. 4:7). And in verse 18 in the same chapter we read that the Jordan resumed its course as soon as the priests who bore the ark of the covenant had come up from the river. *So it is repeatedly stressed that the children of Israel owed the miracle of the crossing over the Jordan to the ark.*

The river of death

The crossing over the Jordan teaches us important lessons as to our union with Christ in His death and resurrection. The ark is a type of Christ, and the Jordan is the river of death. Death is the horizon of our existence here on earth. No man can cross this limit for another, so as to enable him to reach the heavenly home safely. This could only be accomplished by the One who had the power and the authority to lay down His life and to take it again (John 10:18). Because He has cleared a safe passage through the river of death, those who are His own can follow in His steps, though at a respectful distance. Just as the Lord told Peter: "...you cannot follow Me now [through death], but you shall follow Me afterward" (John 13:36; cf. 21:18-22).

Whereas the exodus from Egypt speaks of our deliverance from this present evil age, Israel's entry into Canaan is a type of our having been brought into the heavenly places. Both the Red Sea and the Jordan are types of Christ's death. In the Red Sea crossing the aspects of man's responsibility and of God's judgment are involved. The death of Christ was necessary to rescue us from a world that lies under the wrath of God and from the dominion of the evil one. But in the crossing over the Jordan we see *God's own counsels of grace:* in order to place a heavenly people before Himself He had to raise us up with Christ and to seat us in Him in the heavenly places.

The first truth (the Red Sea crossing) is found particularly in the Epistle to the Romans. We were baptized into the death of *Christ* (Rom. 6) and so we placed ourselves under the authority of our risen Lord – just like the Israelites were baptized into *Moses* in the cloud and in the sea (1 Cor. 10:2). We are no longer under the dominion of the ruler of this world and we can walk in newness of life. We are a pilgrim people on our way to the Promised Land, guided by our great Leader, the Author of our faith. To us, the world has become a wilderness, where God wonderfully provides us with spiritual food and drink. In the midst of a groaning creation we are looking forward to the coming glory, the glorious liberty of the children of God (Rom. 8).

The second truth (the crossing over the Jordan) can be found particularly in the Epistles to the Ephesians and to the Colossians. God wanted to have a people with Himself in heaven and to that end Christ cleared the way through death. He obtained a safe passage for all God's children, who set foot on the other side of the river of death because they are **identified with Christ** – just like the Israelites owed their entry into the land of Canaan by crossing over past the ark of God. For we have been raised up with Christ and have been made to sit together in the heavenly places in Him (Eph. 2:6).

The Old Testament type presents this truth from a practical point of view. The crossing over the Jordan and the filing past the ark in the midst of the river remind us of the fact that God made us alive together with Christ, and raised us up together, and made us sit together in the heavenly places in Christ Jesus. We now are able to set foot on our heavenly inheritance: a "land" full of blessings is accessible to us. We are called to seek and to set our mind on those things which are above, where Christ is, sitting at the right hand of God (Col. 3:1-2). The taking possession of the land of Canaan is a beautiful illustration of this truth. In the same way as Israel had to take the land from the enemy, we have to overcome the evil powers in the heavenly places, that would deny us the possession of our spiritual and eternal blessings in Christ (Eph. 6). Consequently, the Christian does not have to wait for death, in order to reach the land of Canaan. On the contrary, he sets foot on the Promised Land when by faith he identifies himself with Christ and understands that he has been placed in the heavenlies in Him. So he can go in to possess that land – flowing with the eternal blessings God purposed to bestow on His chosen ones – as his present portion.

As to our walk on earth, however, we are still in the wilderness. The blood of the true Passover has secured us from God's wrath (1 Cor. 5:7). And by Christ's death we have also been delivered from the power of sin and Satan. This is shown in type in the Red Sea crossing. Just as the sea separated the redeemed of the Lord from Egypt, so the death of Christ separates us from this present evil world. True, we are still on earth, but here below there is no food for the new life. Our Christian life needs *spiritual* food and drink, and God is providing these in a wonderful way (cf. 1 Cor. 10:3-4).

So we need both types – the Red Sea as well as the Jordan – because they shed light upon the consequences of the death of Christ from different viewpoints. The Red Sea places us in the "wilderness", the Jordan in the "land". Both territories bring their own specific experiences with them. The Christian is familiar with experiences typical of the wilderness as well as with experiences typical of the land. At the Red Sea God's people were delivered by means of Moses' staff – the symbol of God's authority in judging the world. But at the Jordan it was the ark by which they were saved – a type of Christ in His Godhead and manhood. If by faith we follow Him in His steps and believe that we have been made one with Him, who went down for us into the depths of death, we shall realize that He also opened up the entrance for us into "Canaan", the heavenly land that is flowing with milk and honey. None other than this divine Person, the Son of God incarnate, could introduce us into the blessings of heaven. Our hearts are filled with thanks to Him!

The conquest of Jericho

The next incident in Joshua in which the ark played an important part was the conquest of Jericho. Having crossed the Jordan the people camped in Gilgal, near Jericho (Josh. 4:19; 5:10). The city of Jericho was the stronghold of the enemy that now denied the Israelites further entry into the land. If Jericho the mighty would fall, they could march on unhindered.

Measured by human standards, Israel's battle against

Jericho makes strange reading, starting with the preparations recorded in Joshua 5. First, the sons of Israel had to be circumcised; this is a sign of our abandonment of trust in the things of the flesh. In Gilgal the reproach of Egypt was rolled away from them (Josh. 5:9). For the uncircumcised flesh reminded them of the rebellion of all the men who came out of Egypt and of their former state of bondage in the land of Egypt, or to put it in New Testament terms: our bondage under the elements of the world (Gal. 4:3). The Epistle to the Colossians confirms this parallel when it speaks about our being circumcised in Christ (Col. 2:11), and about the resulting duty to put to death our members which are on the earth (Col. 3:5).

The second preparation was that they kept the Passover, the feast commemorating the deliverance from Egypt. We know that Christ, our Passover, was sacrificed for us (1 Cor. 5:7). No matter in what circumstances we are, whether we are in the midst of the trials of the wilderness (cf. Num. 9), or in circumstances in which we enjoy the blessings of our heavenly inheritance, we should always remember the death of our Lord and "keep the Passover" (Josh. 5:10). Then too, we should feed on Him as the risen and glorified Lord in heaven, here typified by the food of the land of Canaan. The manna – the food for the wilderness – ceased after the Israelites had eaten the produce of the land (Josh. 5:11-12).

Having been strengthened in this way, God's people could prepare for battle. We also have a mighty Captain who is leading us, but we must be aware of His holiness. Just as we read in Joshua 5: "I have now come as Commander of the army of the LORD...Take your sandal off your foot, for the place where you stand is holy" (vv. 14-15). This Commander is going before us and **He** is the One who wins the victory, as appears from the next chapter of the Book of Joshua. For the fall of Jericho was nothing less than the work of the ark, that is, of the presence of the Lord Himself (Josh. 6).

The only thing the armed people had to do was to march around the city in silence on six consecutive days. On the

seventh day, however, this silent procession had to go around
the city seven times, the ark always being in the midst of the
procession. The only sound heard was the sound of the rams'
horns before the ark. The people themselves had to keep silent
until the last time they marched around the city on the seventh
day. For the Lord would fight for them and they should hold
their peace. Only on that last great day, after having marched
around the city for the seventh time, they were allowed to raise
a shout of joy – realizing that they owed the victory not to
themselves, but to the ark of God. And then, at the sound of the
trumpets and the shouts of joy of the people the walls of Jericho
fell down flat, leaving this once impregnable fortress open
before the people of God.

Obviously, the meaning of this event to us is: Christ, and
Christ **alone**, has broken the power of the evil one. Thanks to
Christ's triumph Satan is a defeated enemy (cf. John 12:31;
16:11; Acts 2:24; Eph. 4:8-10; Col. 2:15; 2 Tim. 1:10; Heb. 2:14-15;
Rev. 12:11). So we need no longer fear the power of the evil one
– represented in type by the strong fortress of Jericho that
commanded the entry into the Promised Land. This power has
been annihilated by Christ, by His deep humiliation on the
cross, His resurrection from the dead and His triumphal
ascension. The heavenly places, with their riches of spiritual
blessings are lying open before us and we can march on unhindered. We can even consecrate to God's service all those
treasures that used to be under the influence of the evil one
(in the same way as the booty of Jericho was consecrated to the
Lord, Josh. 6:19).

The wiles of the devil

We should still fear, however, the **wiles** of the devil. We need
not be intimidated by his power any more, but we have to arm
ourselves against his temptations. Therefore we are told in
Ephesians 6: "Put on the whole armour of God, that you may
be able to stand against the wiles of the devil" (v. 11). To that
end we need divine weaponry, rather than human; we need the

whole armour of **God**. Let us return now to the Book of Joshua, where we find a clear confirmation of this principle in the chapters following the fall of Jericho. Achan yielded to the wiles of the evil one and took of the accursed things, the things under the ban: a beautiful Babylonian garment, two hundred shekels of silver and a wedge of gold weighing fifty shekels. In his own words, "he coveted them and took them" (Josh. 7:21). This is the cunning work of the evil one, who aims at stimulating and activating the lust of the flesh, the lust of the eyes and the pride of life (1 John 2:16).

The next wile of the devil was self-reliance. After the fall of Jericho the mighty, the Israelites had become self-confident and they believed they could easily conquer Ai, a much smaller town. Apparently, the Lord was not consulted, for we do not read anything of the kind in Joshua 7. It was only after Israel's defeat that Joshua fell to the earth on his face "before the ark of the LORD" (Josh. 7:6). Then he was informed about the sin of Achan, and the mischief he had done was judged.

Then in Joshua 9, we read about the deceit of the Gibeonites. They managed to deceive Joshua and the rulers of the congregation, because the men of Israel "did not ask counsel of the LORD" (v. 14). This is the scheme of acting independently of God and of making friends with His enemies. So we need to be on our guard against all these various wiles of the devil, though we rejoice in the complete victory Christ has won, and have access to the whole realm of heavenly blessings that has been prepared for us.

The ark finds a resting place at Shiloh

After the conquest of Jericho and the destruction of Ai, Joshua and the people marched to Shechem in order to carry out what Moses had commanded the children of Israel much earlier (Josh. 8:30-35; cf. Deut. 11:29-32; 27:1-26). Moses' commandment consisted of three parts:

(1) To set up large stones on Mount Ebal and to write on them a copy of the law of Moses;

(2) To build there an altar of stones, to offer burnt offerings on it and peace offerings, and to eat there and rejoice before the LORD;

(3) To read the blessing on Mount Gerizim and the curse on Mount Ebal.

It is on this solemn occasion the ark of the covenant is mentioned again, for the last time in the Book of Joshua: "Then all Israel, with their elders and officers and judges, stood on either side of the ark before the priests, the Levites, who bore the ark of the covenant of the LORD" (Josh. 8:33). So here again, the ark occupied a central place in the midst of God's people. It was the divine witness of the reading of the law and of the Amen, by which the people once again confirmed their commitment to keep God's statutes (and by which they put themselves under the curse of the law as well, Deut. 27:13-26; Gal. 3:10-13).

Today, we are living in the dispensation of grace. We are no longer under law but under grace (Rom. 6:14). But even now it is true that there is a divine Witness among us, who observes whether we really obey His Word. True enough, those who belong to Christ have been delivered from the eternal curse and have been placed in a position of divine favour – in accordance with God's eternal **counsels** from which nobody can derogate. But as to our walk on earth we are responsible creatures, and we remain subject to God's government. This has to do with God's **ways**, with His righteous rule over us.

Now let us return to the actual history of the ark. For the time being the camp of the Israelites remained at Gilgal, and thus Gilgal was the first station of the ark in the Promised Land. After every campaign of conquest the people returned to the camp at Gilgal. This lasted until most of the land had been subdued before them and there was no good reason against giving the sanctuary **a more central place** in the land.

Shiloh

Then the tabernacle of meeting was set up at Shiloh (Josh. 18:1). We should note that the ark itself is not mentioned by name any more in the Book of Joshua; it is named but once in the Book of Judges. The tabernacle remained in Shiloh until the days of Samuel the prophet. Consequently, Shiloh replaced Gilgal as the place of meeting of the Israelites. Here Joshua arranged, among other things, the further division of the land (Josh. 18-22). Here too, the ark found its first permanent dwelling place in the land of Canaan. We hope to see later on, that the next stay was in Mount Zion, and that the temple of Solomon became the final resting place of the ark.

Shiloh was situated on the mountain range of Ephraim, north of Bethel (Judg. 21:19). The name Shiloh probably means "rest" or "he who brings peace, or prosperity". In Jacob's last words it occurs as the name of a person, obviously a reference to the Messiah: "The sceptre shall not depart from Judah, nor a lawgiver from between his feet, until Shiloh comes; and to Him shall be the obedience of the people [or, the peoples]" (Gen. 49:10).

Judah was the royal tribe. First Chronicles 5:2 tells us that Judah prevailed over his brothers, and that a ruler, namely king David, came from him. But Jacob's prophecy goes beyond that. It alludes to the great Son of David, for He also descended from Judah according to the flesh. To Him would be the obedience of the peoples and nations (nowadays by the obedience of faith and in the coming kingdom by outward submission). His government brings true rest and true peace.

So Shiloh suggests the thought of rest, as well as a state of stability in the country. But the further history of Israel shows that they had a long way to go toward that end. The era of true peace and rest did not come until the reigns of David and Solomon. Generally speaking, the period of the judges was very turbulent. In those times the people of Israel more than once lapsed into rank idolatry and immorality. Their idol worship is depicted as the counterpart of the true worship of the God of Israel in Shiloh (Judg. 18:31).

It is of note indeed, that during this period the ark is mentioned but once, namely in Judges 20:27. In the lives of the people the ark no longer occupied the central place to which it had a right. They did not seek it, as David put it when speaking about the situation in Saul's days (1 Chr. 13:3 NASB). But this holds good for us also: when our attention is no longer focussed on Christ Himself, we may fall into the worst of evils.

Now in Judges 20 there is still another important lesson to be learned about the role of the ark. Not only did it lead the people of God in the battle against the enemies from outside, but it did so too against the evil men who rose up in their very midst and who had to be put away from among them (cf. Deut. 17:7,12; 19:19; 21:21; 1 Cor. 5:13). Similarly, we have no other High Authority than Christ with whom we should take counsel about any conflict that may arise. And especially if fighting against an enemy from **inside** is involved, serious humiliation, a weeping before the Lord is necessary, as well as the awareness that it is a controversy between **brethren** (Judg. 20:26-28).

Then we come to the days of Samuel, the prophet who lived at the end of the period of the judges and at the beginning of the era of the kings. In Samuel's days we still have an established worship at Shiloh and we can assume that the ark stood there for several hundreds of years (from the time of Joshua throughout the period of the judges). True enough, in Judges 20 Bethel (the house of God) is mentioned as the place of residence of the ark, but probably this was just a temporary station, nearer to the scene of battle[1]. According to Judges 21 the camp of the Israelites remained at Shiloh, and so, in the first chapters of First Samuel, this was the spiritual centre of the people and the resting place of the ark, until it was captured by the Philistines.

Note

1. According to some, the coming up of the angel of the LORD from Gilgal
   to Bochim (Judg. 2:1-5) is also to be regarded as a journey of the ark.
   They identify Bochim with Bethel, which in Judges 20:27 is also mentioned as the temporary station of the ark and in Judges 21:2 as a place
   of weeping. In any case, it is important that Bochim (meaning "weeping", or "weepers") speaks of humiliation before God.

The wanderings of the Ark in the days of Samuel

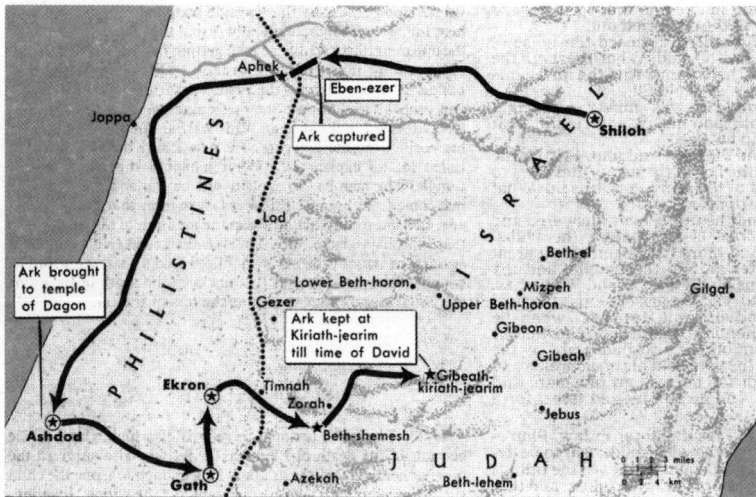

Aphek

Eben-ezer

Ark captured

Joppa

Shiloh

I S R A E L

P H I L I S T I N E S

Lod

Beth-el

Ark brought
to temple
of Dagon

Lower Beth-horon

Mizpeh

Gilgal

Gezer

Upper Beth-horon

Ark kept at
Kiriath-jearim
till time of David

Gibeon

Gibeah

Ekron

Timnah

Gibeath-
kiriath-jearim

Zorah

Jebus

Ashdod

Beth-shemesh

Gath

Azekah

J U D A H

Beth-lehem

miles

km

← Route of the Ark

4

FROM SHILOH TO
MOUNT ZION

Samuel and the ark

Samuel lived at a turning point in the history of Israel, at the time of the transition from the period of the judges to the era of the kings. Actually, he was the link between these two eras. Samuel was the last of the judges, and also the prophet who anointed the first king – and in doing so he appointed him on behalf of the God of Israel.

In the days of the judges everyone did what was right in his own eyes. In those days there was no king in Israel. There was nobody who put affairs in order among the people and thereby strengthened them against their enemies. It was only the grace of God who time and again sent a deliverer when the Israelites cried to Him and turned from their idolatry. The priesthood, this important link between God and the people, had failed as well. The first chapters of 1 Samuel show us how serious the breakdown was, so much so that the priesthood and the service of the house of God had become a mockery.

But then God set to work and He sent His prophet. On the one hand, Samuel had to pass judgment on a situation that God could not bear any longer, on the other hand, he had to be the pioneer of a new regime. Samuel was the herald of the judgment on the priesthood, the house of Eli, but he also introduced the kingship (first that of Saul, the king after the flesh and then that of David, the man after God's own heart). Samuel is called the first of the prophets (cf. Acts 3:24). This does not mean there used to be no other prophets before that. Moses was called a

prophet, and Miriam a prophetess (Ex. 15:20; Deut. 18:15). Even
Abraham was a prophet (Gen. 20:7). So the idea itself was not
unknown, neither was the notion of royalty (cf. Deut. 17; 33:5;
Judg. 8 and 9; 1 Sam. 8). However, with the appearance of
Samuel these duties began to crystallize into permanent insti-
tutions in Israel.

From his earliest days, the life of Samuel was marked out
for the service of the Lord. His mother Hannah had asked him
of the Lord and therefore she also lent him to the Lord. In the
midst of the evil surrounding him, young Samuel ministered
"before the LORD" and grew "before the LORD" (1 Sam. 2:18,21).
Then the moment came when he was called to the service that
God had intended for him. Samuel heard His voice, addressing
him from above the ark, the symbol of God's presence. The
Lord had not spoken for a long time: "And the word of the
LORD was rare in those days; there was no widespread revelation" (1 Sam. 3:1). That was the result of the state of decay and
of spiritual and moral darkness. It was night, in the literal sense
of the word, but also figuratively. Eli the priest was almost
blind. But then all of a sudden God's voice was heard, calling,
"Samuel! Samuel!" It was the first time Samuel heard God's
voice, though he had always been living close to the Lord and
had grown up in His presence. But now the time had come for
him to take up his task as a prophet and to herald a new era, a
new day in the history of God's people. When God spoke,
Samuel readily placed himself at His disposal.

In the calling of Samuel there are important practical lessons
for us and especially for young believers. We too are living in a
time of serious decline. Peter tells us: "For the time has come
for judgment to begin at the house of God" (1 Pet. 4:17). But
then, in the midst of all the evil around us, there is still the
possibility to grow "before the LORD", like Samuel. He always
lived in the presence of God. He even slept in the temple, as the
house of God is called here in 1 Samuel 3:3 (cf. the KJV and
other translations). It appears that around the tent dwelling
more permanent facilities had been built (cf. 1 Sam. 1:9; 2:22;

3:3,15). And there Samuel was **near the ark**, a type of Christ: "Samuel was lying down in the temple of the LORD where the ark of God was" (1 Sam. 3:3 NASB).

What a privilege to live there in God's presence with God speaking to us in a personal way. He has a message for us, both sad and glad. Sad, for God is going to put aside His testimony, in the same way as He rejected His dwelling place in Shiloh. But there are glad tidings as well, for God is announcing the coming of His Anointed, His Christ. He will put everything in order and His glorious reign will bring peace and rest (cf. Ps. 78:56-72).

Maybe we too find it difficult to pass the message of the coming judgment to others, just as Samuel was reluctant to inform Eli about the vision. Yet it is an established fact, as is evidenced by many passages in the New Testament. God has long been patient with His failing Church and the time is coming when it will no longer be His witness on earth. He will judge the unfaithful Church, take up into heaven those who really belong to Him, and then renew His relationship with Israel. After that, Christ will appear in splendour and majesty with His heavenly bride, in order to establish His dominion here on earth and to reign as the Prince of Peace.

The ark captured by the Philistines

After Samuel had been called and had been recognized as a prophet by all Israel, God's judgment was executed upon the house of Eli. Much emphasis is laid on what happened to the ark of God, indicating the importance of this matter. It is an interesting story that clearly shows how God maintained His rights both in relation to His own people and in relation to His enemies.

The essence of these chapters in First Samuel is conveyed by a word of Azariah, one of the later prophets in Judah, who told king Asa: "The LORD is with you while you are with Him.

If you seek Him, He will be found by you; but if you forsake Him, He will forsake you" (2 Chr. 15:2). God was with Israel as long as they walked in His ways. But He could not go with His people when they went astray and turned their backs on Him. They boasted of the privileges they had received from God, in particular of the fact of God's presence among them. That is exactly what they claimed when they used the ark of the covenant as a mascot against the enemy. They treated the ark almost like a good luck charm that would help them in trouble. But it was to no avail, the Israelites were fighting a losing battle. They had forsaken God and He now had to turn away from them. The glory of God was about to leave them because they had forsaken Him.

In fact, both the Israelites and the Philistines made the same mistake, in that they thought the presence of God Himself to be indissolubly linked with the outward sign of it, that is, the ark through which He had demonstrated His presence. When the Israelites suffered their first defeat they sent for the ark from Shiloh in order to secure victory for themselves: "And when the people had come into the camp, the elders of Israel said, 'Why has the LORD defeated us today before the Philistines? Let us bring the ark of the covenant of the LORD from Shiloh to us, that when it comes among us **it may save us** from the hand of our enemies'. So the people sent to Shiloh, that they might bring from there the ark of the covenant of the LORD of hosts, who dwells between the cherubim. And the two sons of Eli, Hophni and Phinehas, were there with the ark of the covenant of God. And when the ark of the covenant of the LORD came into the camp, all Israel shouted so loudly that the earth shook".

But note the reaction of the Philistines: "Now when the Philistines heard the noise of the shout, they said, 'What does the sound of this great shout in the camp of the Hebrews mean?' Then they understood that the ark of the LORD had come into the camp. So the Philistines were afraid, for they said, '**God has come into the camp!**' And they said, 'Woe to us! For such a thing has never happened before. Woe to us! Who will deliver us from the hand of these mighty gods? These are the gods who struck the Egyptians with all the plagues in the wilderness. Be strong and conduct yourselves like men, you Philistines, that you do not become servants of the Hebrews, as they have been to you. Conduct yourselves like men, and fight!' " (1 Sam. 4:3-9).

So the Israelites showed not the slightest sign of humiliation because of their initial defeat, nor did they wonder why it had happened to them. They did not turn from their idols as occurred in 1 Samuel 7, which then was followed by a great victory over the Philistines. No, their reaction was simply: Let us go and fetch the ark, that will help us defeat the enemy. But God did not allow them to use the token of His presence for that purpose! He can never be **forced** by us to intervene! And so the hope for remedy failed. The Israelites suffered a crushing defeat and the ark of God was captured by the Philistines: "So the Philistines fought, and Israel was defeated, and every man fled to his tent. There was a very great slaughter, and there fell of Israel thirty thousand foot soldiers. Also the ark of God was captured; and the two sons of Eli, Hophni and Phinehas, died" (1 Sam. 4:10-11).

No doubt this defeat was very painful for the Israelites. They had boasted that God was with them, but now they had to experience that He had forsaken them. The ark of God was lost, and apparently the sanctuary in Shiloh was destroyed soon after (Ps. 78:60). In his day, the prophet Jeremiah used the putting aside of Shiloh as a telling illustration for the Israelites who boasted of having the temple of the Lord: "The temple of the LORD, the temple of the LORD, the temple of the LORD are these" (Jer. 7:4). No, the prophet said, it is not so. Your conceitedness is wholly out of place. Your worship is just for show, for you are committing all sorts of abominations. Do you think that God will ignore this? What did He do to Shiloh because of the wickedness of His people? He allowed His sanctuary to be destroyed, and the same thing will happen to this temple (Jer. 7:12; 26:6).

So we can draw a parallel between the putting aside of
Shiloh and the later rejection of Israel, which was of an even
more radical nature and marked the beginning of "the times of
the Gentiles" (Luke 21:24). Just as the ark left Shiloh, the glory
of the Lord then withdrew from the temple. Ezekiel witnessed
how the glory of the God of Israel slowly withdrew from
Jerusalem (Ezek. 10 and 11). However, there is yet a gracious
promise for the future. The glory of the Lord will **return** to His
temple in the midst of His people (Ezek. 43), after they have
accepted the Messiah. In connection with this we observe that
the story of the ark has a clear prophetic meaning. The ark was
returned to Israel later on and eventually it was placed by
David – a type of Christ as the Messianic King – on Mount
Zion. This is a shadow of things to come. The theocratic reigns
of David and Solomon point to the coming kingdom of our
Lord Jesus Christ and to His presence in the midst of His
people.

But the story of the ark in 1 Samuel 4 is also important from
a practical point of view for God's people today, for the Church
now being gathered by God from Jews and Gentiles. People
still say: "God is with us!" But this is very often a wrong claim
that is used to conceal all sorts of iniquities, for these men
depreciate both the Scriptures and biblical moral standards. In
such a situation God cannot but turn away from His people
and allow them to be defeated by the advancing enemy, by
humanistic philosophies and evil practices.

Therefore, the story of the capture of the ark should speak
to our hearts as well. Let us show then the same disposition as
Eli, "for his heart trembled for the ark of God" (1 Sam. 4:13).
This makes us feel sympathy for him in spite of all his short-
comings. Unfortunately, his misgivings proved to be true and
the message about the capture of the ark was the immediate
cause of his death. And yet another death was caused by the
sad events of that day: Eli's daughter-in-law went into labour
and as she died she named her child Ichabod (1 Sam. 4:19-22).
This name was a striking expression of the feelings which at

that time filled the hearts of all God-fearing Israelites. Ichabod means **Inglorious**. The glory of God had disappeared from amongst His people. What hope, what expectation was left for Israel now? God's presence was of crucial importance to them. With Him, they were strong, but without Him, they could do nothing. Do we realize this too?

The ark in the country of the Philistines

Now God is not only the Judge of His own people, but also of all the earth. When He punishes His own people, the nations cannot go scot-free. He maintains His rights even with respect to His enemies. This is a general principle in Scripture. But God always **begins** with judging the iniquity of those who enjoy the highest privileges, those who are nearest to Him. To Moses He said: "By those who come near Me I must be regarded as holy" (Lev. 10:3). And Peter says: "For the time has come for judgment to begin at the house of God; and if it begins with us first, what will be the end of those who do not obey the gospel of God?" (1 Pet. 4:17).

This is also illustrated by the story of the ark in Philistine hands. First of all, Israel was judged, then judgment came upon the Philistines. First the **idol** of the Philistines was struck, then both the **people** and the **land** of the Philistines were hard hit. The people in the cities suffered from a plague of tumours, while the land was ravaged by a plague of rats (or, mice). These rodents depleted their food stocks and may have spread the plague among the people. First Samuel 5 mentions only three cities (Ashdod, Gath and Ekron), but the next chapter makes it clear that all the five cities of the Philistines were struck by these plagues (v. 4). The above-mentioned three cities formed a city league together with Ashkelon and Gaza (v. 17); their lords are mentioned in Scripture more than once.

Perhaps the most impressive account is that of the downfall of Dagon, the national deity of the Philistines (in form partly a

man and partly a fish, but according to others the "corn god" of
this people). Having defeated the Israelites, the Philistines took
the ark of God as a trophy from the battle and brought it into
the temple of Dagon. This was an act of homage to their god,
who (so they believed) gave them the victory. But then something curious happened: "And when the people of Ashdod
arose early in the morning, there was Dagon, fallen on its face
to the earth **before the ark** of the LORD" (1 Sam. 5:3). So their
idol had to submit to the God of Israel! Although God's people
were defeated, He Himself emerged victorious. This happened
twice, for they set Dagon in its place again. But then the defeat
of their god was definitive: "And when they arose early the
next morning, there was Dagon, fallen on its face to the ground
before the ark of the LORD. The head of Dagon and both the
palms of its hands were broken off on the threshold; only the
torso of Dagon was left of it" (v. 4).

Thus, the God of Israel who seemingly stood by idly when
His people suffered a defeat (and who had allowed His enemies to capture the ark of the covenant), now showed His great
power and gained a glorious victory. Neither Dagon nor any
other idol made of wood or stone can stand before the living
God. Note that the Philistines always refer to Him as "the God
of Israel". They did not know Him as Yahweh, the covenant
God, who remains for ever faithful to His promises. Another
remarkable thing is that in First Samuel 4:4 He is called "the
LORD of hosts (Yahweh Sabaoth), who dwells between the
cherubim". He, the Commander of the LORD's army, had
forsaken His warriors and had delivered them into the hands
of the enemy. But in spite of that He now showed His power in
the enemy's land.

So the hand of God was very heavy on the Philistines for
seven months and they moved the ark from one place to
another because nobody could endure its presence. Then the
Philistines called for the priests and the diviners, saying, "What
shall we do with the ark of the LORD? Tell us how we should
send it to its place" (1 Sam. 6:2). And the answer of the wise

men was, "If you send away the ark of the God of Israel, do not send it empty; but by all means return it to Him with a trespass offering. Then you will be healed, and it will be known to you why His hand is not removed from you" (v. 3). So they not only had to return the ark, but beyond that they had to pay a trespass or guilt offering to show that they avowed their sin and paid homage to the God of Israel.

The return of the ark to Israel comes up for discussion below. But first it is important for us to see the prophetic and spiritual purport of this story. We have already pointed out that the ark's stay in the country of the Philistines is a prophetic reference to the times of the Gentiles, who particularly at the close of that era will be struck by God's wrath. When God's judgments are in the earth, in the end time, the inhabitants of the world will learn righteousness (Isa. 26:9). The nations will bow before His power and pay homage to Him.

But there is also a spiritual lesson for us. We will recall that the Philistines were of Egyptian origin and had settled in the coastal area of Canaan. They represent worldlings, although they were living in the land of Canaan. These people are on Christian ground so to speak and they claim the "land" which God has promised to His children. But they are not entitled to that heavenly portion because they do not bear the sign of the covenant – usually they are referred to as "the uncircumcised Philistines". Neither have they taken possession of the Promised Land in the way that God had stipulated, i.e., through the Red Sea and the Jordan (both are typical of the death of Christ). The Philistines were the most stubborn enemies of God's people. We hear about them in the days of the patriarchs and finally, it was king David who subdued them.

Therefore, these avowed enemies of Israel are typical of nominal Christians, natural men without true knowledge of the things of God. They boast of their natural resources, of the wisdom of this world and put these things above God's revelation in the Scriptures. When the spiritual state of the people of God is low, the "Philistines" have the upper hand.

There is then a tendency to yield to all sorts of theories of
unbelief. And this predominance can be so strong that one may
hear the reproach, "Do you not know that the Philistines rule
over us?" (Judg. 15:11).

On the other hand, when the authority of Christ is
maintained in the midst of His people and He is given the
preeminence, these evil influences will be checked – in the
same way as the Philistines were overcome by king David.
Furthermore, close contact with the presence of God appears
to be unbearable for these nominal professors. The divine
presence can only bring judgment on them. He overturns their
idols and strikes them with His plagues, just as He once did in
the land of Egypt (cf. 1 Sam. 4:8; 6:6). These afflictions will
cause them to seek ways of getting rid of His presence. But, as
they do so, they will be forced to pay homage to Him – as we
see the Philistines doing when they sent away the ark of the
God of Israel.

The ark returned to Israel

So the ark entered a new stage in its eventful history. Via Beth
Shemesh, a Levitical city not far from Ekron, it returned to
Israel and went to Kirjath Jearim. There it remained until David
gave it a central place once more in the midst of God's people,
when he set up his theocratic reign in Jerusalem.

We have seen how the Philistines learned that the God of
Israel was not to be trifled with. Because the hand of the LORD
was very heavy on them, they understood that His holy presence brought judgment on those who did not know Him. So
they came to the conclusion that they had to return the ark to
its place, to where it belonged – that is, to the land of Israel in
the general sense of the word. Shiloh was not restored as the
centre of worship, for the tabernacle was moved to Nob and
then to Gibeon (cf. 1 Sam. 21:1ff; 1 Chr. 16:39).

But they could not simply return the ark, the symbol of the

divine presence. A satisfaction, a trespass offering had to accompany it. So they made five golden tumours and five golden rats, according to the number of the cities of the Philistines and put them in a chest by the side of the ark (1 Sam. 6:4,8). In this way they brought glory to the God of Israel, acknowledging Him as the Author of the plagues that struck them and pleading with Him for relief.

The Philistines did have their doubts, though, as to whether they really owed all this distress to the presence of the ark or whether it happened to them by chance (v. 9). To them the return of the ark was an experiment. They returned it on a new cart without a driver, drawn by two milk cows. Normally, one would expect these animals to return to their calves. But if that did not happen and the cows took the road to Israel, then this would prove indisputably that the God of Israel had brought the plagues upon them. And indeed, this occurred. Guided supernaturally the cows headed straight for the road to Beth Shemesh (a Levitical city in the territory of Judah that had been given to the Kohathites). They went along the highway, lowing as they went, and did not turn aside to the right hand or the left. And the lords of the Philistines went after them to the border of Beth Shemesh (v. 12). They returned to Ekron only when they saw that the ark was safely received by the men of Beth Shemesh (v. 16). To the Philistines, the matter was now settled and they could only acknowledge the hand of God in all these events.

The use of a new cart to carry the ark and the golden tumours and rats, and cows which had never been yoked, indicated the desire to honour the God of Israel (v. 5). The Philistines put something new and precious at His disposal. Although they certainly did not act according to the Levitical pattern, the law of Moses, too, in some cases required the use of a heifer on which a yoke had never come (Num. 19:2; Deut. 21:3). The offering of the red heifer is a type of the sacrifice of Christ. He was under no obligation to serve, yet He gave Himself as an offering in the prime of life.

The ark at Beth Shemesh and at Kirjath Jearim

I refer to this especially in view of what happened when the ark arrived at Beth Shemesh and was given a warm welcome there: "Now the people of Beth Shemesh were reaping their wheat harvest in the valley; and they lifted their eyes and saw the ark, and rejoiced to see it. Then the cart came into the field of Joshua of Beth Shemesh, and stood there; a large stone was there. So they split the wood of the cart and offered the cows as a burnt offering to the LORD. The Levites took down the ark of the LORD and the chest that was with it, in which were the articles of gold, and put them on the large stone. Then the men of Beth Shemesh offered burnt offerings and made sacrifices the same day to the LORD" (1 Sam. 6:13-15).

This reception of the ark is typical of our attitude towards the Lord Jesus, the true Ark of the covenant. First of all, the people of Beth Shemesh were glad when they saw the ark. They had deplored its absence as the centre of their worship and now they were glad to see it returning to them. This reminds us of the reaction of the disciples when they saw their risen Lord. They were mourning for the passing away of the Lord, but then, all of a sudden, He came and stood in their midst and showed them the signs of His sufferings. John tells us: "He showed them His hands and His side. Then the disciples were glad when they saw the Lord" (John 20:20).

Secondly, worship was restored spontaneously and the ark became the centre of everybody's attention. The Levites gave the ark a place of honour on a large stone. Then the cows which had been hitched to the cart were offered as a burnt offering to the Lord, possibly on the same large stone, which then served as an altar (cf. Judg. 13:19). Further, other burnt offerings and sacrifices (that is, peace offerings) are mentioned in verse 15. The burnt offerings were wholly consumed by fire and were intended for God only, but of the peace offerings the Israelites were allowed to eat (except the fat).

So the return of the ark gave rise to a happy sacrificial meal.

This goes for us too, when Christ is recognized as the true Centre of gathering and He is given the preeminence. As the risen One He will then show us the marks of His sufferings and He will lead the songs of praise in the midst of His brethren. Then we shall offer up spiritual sacrifices and we shall rejoice in the fellowship which we have with the Father and the Son, and with one another.

The story of the return of the ark, however, took a serious turn after the men of Beth Shemesh abandoned their initial reverent attitude towards the ark and wanted to have a closer look at it. They failed to remember that the ark was the holiest object of their worship, the throne of God Himself. Probably driven by curiosity, they looked into the ark (v. 19). But then God showed Himself to be the holy One and He struck the men of Beth Shemesh, just as later on He struck Uzzah for his error, when he took hold of the ark (2 Sam. 6:6-7). It was unforgivable to touch or to watch the holy vessels (cf. Num. 4:15,20).

So their joy turned to grief and they lamented because the LORD had struck them with a great slaughter (at least seventy people died, see JND, NIV). The presence of the ark became unbearable to them: "And the men of Beth Shemesh said, 'Who is able to stand before this holy LORD God? And to whom shall it go up from us?' So they sent messengers to the inhabitants of Kirjath Jearim, saying, 'The Philistines have brought back the ark of the LORD; come down and take it up with you' " (vv. 20-21). Deeply impressed by the LORD's holiness, they went to the other extreme and feared to retain the ark with them. Their conduct was much the same as that of the Philistines in the previous chapter, who sent the ark from one place to another because they could not bear its presence.

A New Testament parallel to this is the account of the Gergesenes, who begged the Lord to depart from their region after He had dealt with them with severity (Matt. 8:34). Only later on they learned to appreciate the blessing of the Lord's presence (Matt. 14:34-36). Both blessing and judgment accompany the divine presence. **Blessing** when we answer to His

thoughts, but **judgment** when we derogate from His rights.
The wish to look into the ark can be compared with the desire
to fathom the mystery of Christ's Person. But it is a divine pre-
rogative to understand the union of His Godhead and manhood. No one knows the Son except the Father (Matt. 11:27),
and we are only allowed to contemplate Him with the utmost
reverence!

However, the ark did reach a safe haven in Kirjath Jearim,
a few miles west of Jerusalem. This town was situated higher
up in the mountains and therefore the messengers from Beth
Shemesh could say: "...come down and take it up with you".
Here, the ark got a place of honour at the highest point in town,
the house of Abinadab on the hill. Further, it received special
attention there: "...and [they] consecrated Eleazar his son to
keep the ark of the LORD" (1 Sam. 7:1). The keeping of the ark
probably means **guarding** it, so that henceforth it would be
preserved from indiscreet looks or actions.

The ark remained in this safe and separate place for a long
time, for about seventy years: first the twenty years mentioned
in 1 Samuel 7:2, then the entire reign of king Saul (forty years
according to Acts 13:21), and then at least the seven years of
David's reign in Hebron. It would seem that Samuel did not
make any attempt to return the ark to the centre of the religious
life of God's people. Perhaps he realized that the time was not
yet ripe for it and that this would be one of the duties of the
anointed king. This is the next thing we shall consider. King
Saul, however, failed to do this[1].

The ark brought up to Mount Zion

Unquestionably the bringing up of the ark to Mount Zion
marks a peak in its history. It was king David, the man after
God's own heart, who put the ark once again in the centre of
Israel's worship. At last it arrived in the place where God chose
to make His name abide, the place of which Moses had spoken

long ago (cf. Deut. 12). This ushered in a completely new era. The central place of worship on Mount Zion was now linked with the new seat of David's government over the people of Israel. Initially, David was anointed king over the house of Judah only. But gradually all the people rallied behind him and he was anointed king over all Israel at Hebron (2 Sam. 5:1-5). Then he began to look for a new, more centrally situated seat of government, which he found in Jerusalem – the city of the former king and priest Melchizedek (Gen. 14:18).

David took the stronghold of Zion, to the south of the city, and made it his residence, the City of David (2 Sam. 5:7). Later on the name Zion was used for the whole of Jerusalem – referring to it as the city of God, the city of the great King (Ps. 48:1-2). Not only **David** but also **the Lord** had chosen Zion for His habitation (Ps. 132:13-14). But it is good to see that David took the initiative to make Zion God's dwelling place. When David realized that the Lord had established him as king over all Israel and had exalted his kingdom, he did not want to reign without Him. He desired to be a king by divine right, because he knew that he owed his kingship to Him. He wished to reign with God's help and to maintain God's rights over His people. It was not David's throne that mattered, but the throne of the Lord (cf. 1 Chr. 29:23). Zion was both the seat of God's government and the centre of Israel's worship.

This turning point in the history of Israel offers some rich prophetic and spiritual lessons. Primarily, it is a **prophetic** reference to the coming kingdom of our Lord Jesus Christ, who must reign till He has put all enemies under His feet (1 Cor. 15:25). But in a **spiritual** sense His reign takes shape among His people already now. If Christ is recognized as Lord and Master, God's kingdom will be seen as a reality in our lives. The features of God's kingdom are: "...righteousness and peace and joy in the Holy Spirit" (Rom. 14:17). That which will be revealed publicly on the earth at Christ's return, is today the portion of those who have been translated into the kingdom of the Son of God's love, the Man after God's own heart

It was a joyful day when the ark was brought to Jerusalem. God's throne found a suitable resting place and David reigned over Israel by divine right. In the same way it is a matter of great joy to us when Christ finds a dwelling place in the midst of His own, and His divine authority is recognized by all.

(Col. 1:13). The peace of God fills our hearts; we recognize His rights and we seek His righteousness; and we also rejoice in God by the power of the Holy Spirit. But we will enjoy these blessings in a practical way only by recognizing the authority of God's Anointed. Christ must be at the centre of our lives and He must be able to dwell in our midst. Just as we see this in type in the life of king David: the authority of the anointed king had to be recognized **and the ark** with which God had linked His presence had to be given its proper, central place in the worship of God's people. This Old Testament type also demonstrates that this involves both personal and collective privileges and duties. These matters concern all the people of God.

In the light of this let us look at the account of the bringing up of the ark to Mount Zion, as it is recorded in Second Samuel 6 and First Chronicles 13, 15 and 16. The main lesson is that Christ should find a resting place in the midst of His own, a permanent dwelling place connected with a worship according to God's will. God can rest only there where His rights are owned and where people wholeheartedly submit to His authority. The fulfilment of this condition is essential, for David was first honoured as king and only then the ark was brought to its resting place on Mount Zion.

When we read these chapters the joyfulness of the event should strike us. This is particularly stressed in First Chronicles. The entry of the ark into the City of David was accompanied by music, dancing and songs of joy. This was suitable for the earthly people of God. To us who worship God in spirit and truth (John 4:24; Phil. 3:3), these things have a **spiritual** meaning. What is important is joy in the Holy Spirit. The same applies to the sacrifices that were offered on the occasion of the bringing up of the ark: our duty is to offer up **spiritual** sacrifices (1 Pet. 2:5).

It is remarkable that the New Testament does not mention the use of musical instruments in Christian worship. The only thing mentioned is **singing**, the singing of psalms and hymns and spiritual songs (Eph. 5:19; Col. 3:16). And then Scripture

adds that it should be a singing in our hearts to the Lord. In
other words, the singing should not be lip service, but it should
have an inner value and reality in God's sight. Now it **is** a
matter of great joy for us when we realize that God wants to
dwell among us in the Person of His Son. The lesson of this Old
Testament type is: Do we really give Him the place which is
due to Him, a resting place, a place of honour? Is Christ truly
the Centre of our worship and are we in the place according to
His mind? And further: Do we recognize His authority as
God's Anointed, and the rule He wants to manifest through
His Spirit (1 Cor. 12:11)?

The Epistle to the Hebrews teaches us that the Israelites
who lived at the time of king David were not the only ones who
were allowed to come to Mount Zion – in a solemn procession,
with the ark in their midst. Indeed, this has a deeper meaning
and it is a privilege still valid today. For we as Christians have
not come to Mount Sinai, but we "have come to Mount Zion
and to the city of the living God, the heavenly Jerusalem" (Heb.
12:22). Mount Zion was the mountain of God's **grace**. After a
long succession of failures to honour Him, He gave them king
David. This was an act of God's grace. For Israel, this meant a
new beginning, a period of unprecedented blessing. Zion was
a token of this, for God had chosen it as His dwelling place. On
Mount Zion we do not see a people afraid to draw near to God,
a people under the curse of the law (as once on Mount Sinai).
Here we see a people full of joy, rejoicing in the anointed king
and in God Himself. There is no fear in His presence.

As Christians we know that we have been translated into
the kingdom of the Son of God's love and that His rule is a
gracious one. Under His reign we are happy and free. We
rejoice in His presence and we have free access to God. We are
blessed with spiritual and heavenly blessings. We have not
been brought to an earthly but to a heavenly city, the Jerusalem
above (Gal. 4:26). We share in the privileges of the coming
kingdom, so that we do not fear, but are full of joy in the
presence of God and His Anointed. We praise His name, which

very soon will be excellent in all the earth, in our songs of praise and adoration.

There are still some details to which we should pay attention before going further. The first attempt to bring the ark into the City of David failed, because God's holiness was not sufficiently taken into account. The ark ought to be carried on the shoulders of the Levites; it was not to be transported on a cart (Num. 7:9). Nor were the Levites permitted to touch the ark and the other holy vessels. When the priests had covered them with several coverings and had inserted their poles, the sons of Kohath came to carry them. But they were not allowed to touch any holy thing, lest they died (Num. 4:15-20). Both instructions were disregarded. For David had the ark transported on a new cart, and Uzzah put out his hand to the ark of God and took hold of it. The judgment announced in Numbers 4 was fulfilled and Uzzah died on the spot[2].

So if it is our sincere desire that God should dwell in our midst, it is necessary to take account of His holy demands. We should not forget that He is the Holy One and that His revealed will should be the pattern of our worship. We cannot act like the Philistines, who returned the ark to Israel on a new cart. For other parts of the tabernacle the use of carts was allowed, but for the holy vessels it was not, let alone for the most holy object: the ark, the throne of God, the LORD of hosts (2 Sam. 6:2). This proves that human inventions are not needed in bearing the testimony with which God has entrusted us. When we present God's excellencies and the glories of the Lord Jesus Christ to this world, our duties can be fulfilled only by the power of God and of His Spirit. The carrying on the shoulders also points to the necessity of suitable reverence.

It is comforting to see that the presence of the ark not only caused judgment, but also **blessing**. This was the experience of Obed-Edom the Gittite, in whose house the ark remained for three months. After Uzzah's death the king was afraid to give it a dwelling place in the City of David. It is remarkable that a stranger, a Philistine, then should become host to the ark, and

be blessed (cf. Eph. 2:19). We read that he was blessed because
of the ark of God (2 Sam. 6:12); in other words, he was blessed
because of a life in God's presence. And the blessing experienced by Obed-Edom and all his household (v. 11), encouraged
David and so he decided to bring up the ark from the house of
Obed-Edom with joy.

This second time things went much better. The instructions
of Moses were observed, for the Levites bore the ark of God on
their shoulders, by its poles (1 Chr. 15:2,15). King David also
spoke to the leaders of the Levites to appoint singers, musicians
and doorkeepers for the ark. Obed-Edom became one of the
doorkeepers; he did not want to part with the ark to which he
owed so much blessing. The task of these guardians of the ark
was to ensure that it was not touched by unholy objects or
persons. Furthermore, offerings were offered for the success of
the journey:

(1) after the first six paces (2 Sam. 6:13);

(2) on the way because it was plain that God was with the
Levites as they carried out their duties (1 Chr. 15:26);

(3) and finally, in acknowledgment of a safe arrival at their
destination (1 Chr. 16:1). There David set up a regular worship
before the ark in Zion; we hope to say more about this in the
next chapter.

But there was one person who did not partake in the public
merrymaking: Michal the daughter of Saul, the man who had
not bothered about the ark. When she saw David rejoicing
before the ark, she despised him in her heart. She could not
appreciate his priestly activities before the LORD. It is a sad
ending of this happy story, which contains a serious warning to
us in our day, to beware lest there be in any of us an evil heart
of unbelief in departing from the living God (Heb. 3:12).

Notes

1. According to First Chronicles 13:3 God's people did not seek the ark in the days of Saul (NASB). Yet in First Samuel 14:18 we read that Saul took the ark with him in the battle against the Philistines. The problem is in the manuscripts, but there seem to be good reasons to believe that not the ark but the ephod is meant here. The ephod is already mentioned in verse 3, and Saul's commandment to the priest in verse 19 apparently also alludes to this priestly vestment. Ahijah had to withdraw his hand out of the breastplate of judgment, which contained the Urim and the Thummim. In any case, here again, Saul was too impatient to wait for the Lord.

2. According to Second Samuel 6 this happened near Nachon's threshing floor, according to First Chronicles 13 near that of Chidon. Some explain this difference by the suggestion that Chidon was the new owner of the threshing floor at the time of writing of the Chronicles. The name of the place was changed to Perez Uzzah, that is, "Outburst against Uzzah".
It is also remarkable that this serious event took place near a threshing floor. This reminds us of what happened on the threshing floor of Araunah the Jebusite (called "Ornan" in First Chronicles) years later. That was the critical point where the plague was stayed, thanks to the offerings sacrificed by David on the altar he had erected there. It was there, too, that the temple was built. In Scripture, the threshing floor is always linked with purging, with separating good from evil, and the chaff from the wheat (cf. Matt. 3:12).

5

FROM MOUNT ZION TO
MOUNT MORIAH

The worship before the ark on Mount Zion

When the ark had reached its resting place on Mount Zion, they set it in the midst of the tabernacle that David had erected for it. Then they offered burnt offerings and peace offerings **before God**, in appreciation of the successful journey from the house of Obed-Edom (1 Chr. 16:1). Thereupon David blessed the people in the name of the LORD, who had entered His dwelling place in Zion and had established His throne there (v. 2). The king also prepared a feast for all the people: "Then he distributed to everyone of Israel, both man and woman, to everyone a loaf of bread, a piece of meat, and a cake of raisins" (v. 3). Zion was the place of blessing, where the poor among the people were satisfied with bread (cf. Ps. 132:15).

Zion was also the place of worship. It was a daily worship taking place **before the ark**, to commemorate, to thank, and to praise the LORD God of Israel (v. 4ff.). Henceforth, the ark with which God had linked His presence was to remain the focus of attention. It was not again to sink into oblivion, as had happened during its long stay at Kirjath Jearim. Worship before the ark as instituted by king David consisted mainly of music and singing, because for the time being the sacrificial service took place before the tabernacle of the LORD at the high place that was at Gibeon (vv. 39-40). This dual service of worship continued until the completion of the temple.

The author of First Chronicles also gives the wording of the hymn that on this glad day of the entry of the ark was sung for the first time. It is a combination of verses from several Psalms (Psalms 105, 96 and 106), and they are of a teaching and prophetic character. David's song of thanksgiving celebrates God's wondrous works in the history of Israel and also His universal glory as the Creator and Judge of all the earth. The LORD reigns, and He is coming to judge the earth (vv. 31-33). This will be for the benefit of His people who will then be gathered together and delivered from the Gentiles (v. 35). Thus, the prophetic perspective of this song reaches to the end time, when Israel's elect will be gathered together from the four winds, from one end of heaven to the other (cf. Matt. 24:30-31).

But this chapter (1 Chr. 16) also contains much teaching in relation to our gathering together as believers in the present time. Here we see a people gathered together **around the ark**. This speaks of Christ as the true Centre of His own who gather together around Him. All attention is focussed on our blessed Lord. He is the Centre of blessing and we bring our offerings, our praise and worship before Him. But then He also speaks to us. Under the guidance of His Spirit a prophetic ministry of the Word of God is taking place, with a view to honouring God and teaching His people. In connection with this it is important to note that the singers **prophesied** with their musical instruments (1 Chr. 25:1-3). And they did so according to the order of the king.

The service of the singers and the musicians as instituted by king David after the ark had reached its resting place in Zion (1 Chr. 6:31), points to a prophetic voicing of divine truth. There-fore, it is not merely by chance that the apostle Paul compares the ministry of the Word in the local gathering to the playing of musical instruments (1 Cor. 14:7). Every instrument has its own distinct sound. Likewise, the ministry of the Word should have a recognizable and understandable nature, depending on the instrument that the Holy Spirit is using. God has given differ-ent gifts in the Church, but they should render the whole of the truth together and in harmony. Do we know such a prophetic ministry of God's Word around Christ as our Centre?

The ark and the temple site

Although the ark had reached its resting place in Zion, it still remained under tent curtains, whereas David himself dwelt in a house of cedar. David realized that there was something wrong in this. The ark, the throne of the LORD, should have a dwelling place at least as magnificent as the palace of the king (2 Sam. 7:2; 1 Chr. 17:1). So David discussed the matter with Nathan the prophet, who entirely agreed with the king and told him, "Do all that is in your heart, for God is with you".

But in that same night the word of God came to Nathan with a different message: it was not David who would build a house for the LORD (in the sense of a permanent **dwelling place**), but the LORD who would build a house for him (in the sense of a permanent **dynasty**). So things were exactly the other way round. God is no man's debtor. Besides, heaven is His throne and the earth His footstool. And had He ever in the history of Israel dwelt in a house of cedar? No, the LORD would first make David a house and would set up his "seed" after him (that is, king Solomon), and then the latter would build Him a house. Beyond this we can also discern something else in this prophecy concerning David's seed: the promise of the Messiah that was to come, great David's greater Son (but above all the Son of the Father, and daily His delight).

There was yet another argument which the LORD used to keep David from building the temple: he had shed much blood on the earth in His sight (1 Chr. 22:8). David was a man of war, but his son would be a man of rest. It would be better if a "man of rest" were to build a "house of rest" for the ark of the covenant (cf. 1 Chr. 22:9 with 28:2-3). This task was to be accomplished by David's son and the rest and peace that would mark his reign were even expressed in his name. Solomon means "peaceful", or "rich in peace". This prince of peace was to build the permanent dwelling place of the ark, even though David was permitted to make the necessary preparations for its building, furnishing and worship (see 1 Chr. 22-29).

David also received a divine indication of where the temple, the house of rest for the ark, was to be built. But unlike all the plans in connection with the temple, which David received by divine revelation (1 Chr. 28:19), the indication of the temple site came about through serious problems. The story is well-known. David allowed himself to be moved by Satan to number Israel. Perhaps he wished to boast of the strength of his army. But even to Joab, the commander of the army, the king's commandment to number the people was abominable. But above all, it was an evil thing in God's sight, for He resists the proud, but gives grace to the humble. David did repent, it is true, but too late for him to get off cheaply. He was allowed to choose one of three judgments for himself, and he chose to fall into the hand of the LORD.

So the LORD sent a plague upon Israel and seventy thousand men of the people died. But when the angel stretched out his hand over Jerusalem, the LORD relented from the destruction and said to the angel that destroyed among the people, "It is enough; now restrain your hand". At that moment, the angel was by the threshing floor of Araunah (or Ornan) the Jebusite. David, his eyes on the angel who was striking the people, confessed his sin and interceded on behalf of Israel. The divine answer was that only a substitutionary sacrifice could bring relief and it was to be offered on the threshing floor where the angel stood. So there David built an altar to the LORD, and offered burnt offerings and peace offerings and called on the LORD; and He answered him from heaven by fire on the altar of burnt offering. Then the LORD commanded the angel and he returned his sword into its sheath.

The plague having been stayed in this way, David spoke the memorable words: "**This** is the house of the LORD God, and **this** is the altar of burnt offering for Israel" (1 Chr. 22:1). It was the place where judgment was turned away and where a substitutionary sacrifice satisfied God's holy demands. This was the right place for God's house in the midst of His people and for the altar of burnt offering for Israel. Here God had revealed His holiness, but also the exceeding riches of His grace. It was here He could dwell, in the place that was the symbol of judgment as well as of grace, of punishment as well as of atonement.

Moreover, from 2 Chronicles 3:1 it appears that this place was in the Mount of the LORD, that is, Mount Moriah. Now this would link it with Genesis 22, where the **land** of Moriah is mentioned. Abraham had to offer his only son Isaac, his most treasured possession, on one of the mountains of which God would tell him. But there, in the Mount of the LORD, He provided for Himself the lamb for a burnt offering. Prophetically, this pointed to Christ, God's only begotten Son, who was foreordained before the foundation of the world to be the Lamb of God. Abraham could spare his son. God could **not** spare His own Son, but delivered Him up for us all (Rom. 8:32). The Son of God was the true sacrificial Lamb that made atonement for all the sins of God's people.

So this place of sacrifice was perfectly appropriate to be the site of the altar of burnt offering and of the future temple. But it was some time before it was put into use as such, and the ark could find its final resting place in the temple. In First Chronicles the preparations for the building of the temple follow immediately upon the story of the fixing of the place of the temple and of the altar of burnt offering. But these preparations seem to have taken considerable time, for Solomon worked on the construction of the temple for seven years from the fourth year of his reign (1 Ki. 6:37,38; 2 Chr. 3:2).

For the time being, the ark remained in its place on Mount Zion. Thus it was still separated from the other holy vessels, that were in the tabernacle at the high place in Gibeon. The ark, the tabernacle of meeting and all the holy things were only brought into the temple after it had been finished in the eleventh year of Solomon's reign. Till then the king continued to sacrifice at the high place that was at Gibeon and also before the ark in the City of David, which is Zion (1 Ki. 3:4, 15; 8:1-4).

Other references to the ark in Second Samuel

Now we have to go back in the history of Israel, because Second Samuel mentions some other events in relation to the ark, that are not found in First Chronicles. David's desire to build a house for the ark of the LORD is found in both Books; so is the account of the census that led to the decision about the place of the future temple. But the sad story of Uriah and the rebellion of Absalom are given only in Second Samuel, *and in both accounts we also read something about the ark of the covenant.*

In Chronicles the history of God's people is recorded from the point of view of God's sovereign grace. But in the earlier historical Books it is more the line of man's responsibility that is emphasized. Therefore, David's adultery with Bathsheba and all its painful consequences are found only in Second Samuel. In an attempt to conceal his sin, David had Uriah sent back from the battlefield. But Uriah could not be persuaded to go to his own house. He said to David, "**The ark** and Israel and Judah are dwelling in tents, and my lord Joab and the servants of my lord are encamped in the open fields. Shall I then go to my house to eat and drink, and to lie with my wife? As you live, and as your soul lives, I will not do this thing" (2 Sam. 11:11). We can conclude from these words that the ark accompanied the Israelites in the war against the Ammonites. Should not David have been there, too? Then he would not have failed so miserably. It is good to see that Uriah mentions the ark first of all. This would teach us that in all things **Christ** should have the preeminence (cf. Col. 1:18). His interests must come first.

When David escaped from Absalom his son, the ark is mentioned again. Absalom had himself proclaimed king in Hebron and most Israelites sided with him. David had to leave Jerusalem. But some people remained loyal to him and followed him, among them Zadok the priest and the Levites bearing the ark. But David decided not to take the ark with him. The king said to Zadok, "Carry **the ark of God** back into the city. If I find favour in the eyes of the LORD, He will bring me back and show me both it and His habitation. But if He says thus: 'I have no delight in you', here I am, let Him do to me as seems good to Him" (2 Sam. 15:25-26).

No doubt David had to go a very difficult way. Yet he totally confided in God and put everything into His hands. If it was God's will to restore him in his royal powers, then this would surely happen and he would see the ark again. If not, it would be all right too. He knew that the Lord went with him, even though the visible sign of His presence did not accompany him. The ark had to remain in its place. For the throne of God cannot be moved, no matter what plans man devises.

The ark brought into the temple

Now let us follow the ark at the last stage of its journey, from Mount Zion to Mount Moriah. The final destination of the ark was the temple of Solomon, the "house of rest for the ark of the covenant of the LORD, and for the footstool of our God" (1 Chr. 28:2). The time of its wanderings had come to an end now. No longer should it lead the people to victory in their battles, for the enemies had been overcome and rest and peace prevailed in Israel. The ark took up its final resting place, not in a tent dwelling – a temporary habitation – but in the temple, a permanent residence.

The temple of Solomon was therefore marked by great contrasts to the tabernacle. Everything spoke of durability and of royal splendour. It was built of quarried stone and cedar and cypress timber and a vast amount of precious metals was used to decorate it. The temple was twice as large as the tabernacle in the wilderness. There was also a vestibule in front of the sanctuary and wings consisting of three floors with a height of five cubits abutted on the main walls. Here were the storehouses and the treasuries.

Other significant differences were:

(1) The two bronze pillars in front of the temple, called Jachin ("He shall establish") and Boaz ("in Him is strength"). Their capitals were adorned with networks and rows of pomegranates. There were no such pillars before the tabernacle.

(2) The Sea of cast bronze, standing on twelve oxen, instead of the former laver for the priests.

(3) Ten lavers on carts of bronze, to wash such things as they offered for the burnt offering (or possibly the utensils for the burnt offerings).

(4) Ten lampstands of gold, instead of the one lampstand in the tabernacle.

(5) Ten tables of gold for the showbread, instead of the one table in the tabernacle.

(6) Two doors of olive wood for the entrance of the inner sanctuary and two doors of cypress wood for the main room of the temple. They replaced the veils, although in 2 Chronicles 3:14 mention is still made of a veil for the Most Holy Place. Probably the doors were open and then the veil would still separate the main room from the inner room.

(7) Two courts with a surrounding stone wall (one court for the priests and one for the people), in contrast to the one court of the tabernacle that was surrounded by a fence of fine linen.

(8) Finally, in the Most Holy Place two gigantic cherubim, fashioned by carving, and overlaid with gold. The total wingspan of the cherubim was twenty cubits. They "spread their wings, and overshadowed the ark of the covenant of the LORD" (1 Chr. 28:18). We do not find these in the tabernacle.

The last mentioned feature is important for our subject. Why these two wooden cherubim above the ark when there were two cherubim of gold on it already, arising from the mercy seat? Why, we could further ask ourselves, do we find so many carved cherubim in the decorations of the temple, whereas they were scarce in the tabernacle? Maybe the answer is found in the fact that the cherubim in Scripture are closely connected with the realization of God's government. What is more appropriate in the theocratic reign of Solomon than these guardians of the theocracy?

Another interesting thing is that these cherubim in the inner sanctuary did not face the mercy seat, as did the cherubim of gold above the ark itself (although the Most Holy Place is specifically called "the place of the mercy seat", 1 Chr. 28:11). The cherubim of olive wood that with their large wings filled almost the entire room, "faced inward" (2 Chr. 3:13), that is, they faced the main room of the temple. In other words, their eyes were turned towards the outside world in order to maintain the rights of God's throne there; for in the kingdom of peace righteousness must reign in all the earth. The cherubim made one think of a chariot, which served as the basis for God's throne (1 Chr. 28:18; cf. Ps. 18:10 and Ezek. 1). Thus, the ark of the covenant found its final resting place in Solomon's temple, under the shadow of these cherubim.

The ark's entry into the temple is described in First Kings 8 and Second Chronicles 5. It appears from everything that it was a solemn and at the same time a particularly festive event. The ark reached its resting place on the occasion of the dedication of the temple, which took place during the Feast of Tabernacles in the seventh month: "Solomon assembled the elders of Israel and all the heads of the tribes, the chief fathers of the children of Israel, in Jerusalem, that they might bring the ark of the covenant of the LORD up from the City of David, which is Zion. Therefore all the men of Israel assembled together with the king at the feast, which was in the seventh month" (2 Chr. 5:2-3).

The Levites duly performed their duties and brought up the ark, together with the tabernacle of meeting, and all the holy furnishings that were in the tabernacle. The king and all the congregation of Israel participated in a service before the ark: they sacrificed sheep and oxen that could not be counted or numbered for multitude. Then, the priests carried the ark into the inner sanctuary and placed it under the wings of the cherubim. The priests came out again and meanwhile, all the Levitical singers began to praise the LORD with the chorus: "For He is good, for His mercy endures for ever". And it came to

At last, the arks found a permanent resting place and was no longer a burden on the shoulders of the Levites. This is a prophetic reference to the rest of the coming kingdom, but it is also true today that Christ desires to find a permanent resting place with His own. And this is the case if He, as the true Prince of peace, can come to a spiritual temple that answers to the mind of God.

pass when the priests came out of the Most Holy Place, and the singers lifted up their voice and praised the LORD, that the house was filled with a cloud. The glory of the LORD filled the temple, and He sat down on the throne that had been prepared for Him. From now on, this would be His habitation, the resting place of the LORD and the ark of His strength (2 Chr. 6:41).

The ark's entry into the temple means much to us, too, for the temple is a type of the Church of the living God. Coming to Christ as to a living Stone, we also, as living stones, are being built up a spiritual house, a holy priesthood, to offer up spiritual sacrifices acceptable to God through Jesus Christ (1 Pet. 2:4-5). And Paul reminds the Corinthians of the same truth: "Do you not know that you are the temple of God and that the Spirit of God dwells in you?" (1 Cor. 3:16). Therefore, the typical meaning of this story for us as Christians consists of three lessons:

(1) God desires to dwell in His temple, the place of His throne.

(2) He wants us to give Christ (the Ark) the central place that is due to Him alone.

(3) Then His Spirit can really fill the house.

In relation to this two more remarks can be made. First of all, the Old Testament types serve as illustrations for the realization of the truth in our daily lives. Consequently, the fact that the cloud filled the house after the ark had been carried to its place, not only speaks of the descent of the Holy Spirit on the day of Pentecost, but also of **the practical enjoyment** of this glorious fact. The Spirit will work in our midst as Christ receives the place of honour that only He is entitled to.

Secondly, the temple and the tabernacle have different meanings. It is true, both of them are types of the Church as a spiritual house, but this is shown from different viewpoints. The tabernacle was a **temporary** dwelling for the journey through the wilderness, the temple was a **permanent** resting place in the Promised Land. Another point is that the temple was not built until rest and peace prevailed in the land and king Solomon reigned as the prince of peace. Likewise, God's dwelling in our midst will be realized insofar as we take possession of our inheritance in the heavenly places (cf. Eph. 1 and the end of Eph. 2), and as Christ is ruling in our hearts as the Prince of Peace (cf. the prayer in Eph. 3).

The final part of the ark's story

Lastly, we would like to say something about the further history of the ark as we find it in the Old Testament. The small amount of information we have about this in Scripture, apart from some Psalms referring to the ark, is notable. Perhaps this has to do with the decline that set in before the end of Solomon's reign.

In any case, in times of **revival**, namely under Hezekiah and Josiah, we do hear something about the ark. Hezekiah spread the letter which he received from the king of Assyria before the LORD and addressed his prayer to the "LORD God of Israel, the One who dwells between the cherubim" (2 Ki. 19:15). And Josiah called the ark by its name when he encouraged the Levites to serve at the celebration of the Passover (2 Chr. 35:3). From this verse some gather that the ark was removed from the temple for some time, but we cannot know this for certain. The words of Josiah can also be understood as the observation of a fact. Because the ark found a resting place in the temple, it was no longer a burden on the shoulders of the Levites and so they could devote themselves to other tasks according to the written instructions of David and Solomon.

It seems likely that the ark was destroyed when Jerusalem was captured by Nebuzaradan the captain of the guard. For he burned the house of the LORD and the entire city with fire (2 Ki. 25:8-9). However, according to 2 Chronicles 36:18, the Chaldeans took all the treasures of the house of the LORD to Babylon. But some believe that the ark was buried by Jeremiah the prophet and others that it was carried away to Ethiopia. But these speculations do not contribute to a better insight into its typical meaning. In the end, the ark itself was nothing more than the outward sign of the divine presence.

The shadows must flee when the reality, which is found in Christ, has come (cf. Col. 2:17). Jeremiah referred to this when he spoke about the restoration of Israel in the last days: "Then it shall come to pass, when you are multiplied and increased in the land in those days", says the LORD, "that they will say no more, 'The ark of the covenant of the LORD'. It shall not come to mind, nor shall they remember it, nor shall they visit it, nor shall it be made anymore. At that time Jerusalem shall be called The Throne of the LORD, and all the nations shall be gathered to it, to the name of the LORD, to Jerusalem; they shall walk no more after the stubbornness of their evil heart" (Jer. 3:16-17).

But this holds good for us already now. We do not need an outward symbol of God's presence, because God's Spirit dwells in the Church and in its individual members. The presence of the Holy Spirit is not dependent on any ceremonial. But the prophecy of Jeremiah will be fulfilled literally at the coming of the Lord. When Jerusalem shall be called The Throne of the LORD, and the name of the city shall also be: THE LORD IS THERE (Ezek. 48:35), there shall be no need for an ark as the throne of the LORD.

For that reason we do not find an ark in the Most Holy Place in Ezekiel's temple. Indeed, the sanctuary as described by Ezekiel seems to be almost vacant. The only object we read of is a wooden **altar** in the holy place, which at the same time is called the **table** that is before the Lord (Ezek. 41:22). This altar-table unites the aspects of worship and fellowship in God's presence and this typical function seems to be its sole purpose.

The New Testament contains only three references to the ark and the mercy seat (Rom. 3:25; Heb. 9:4-5; Rev. 11:19). We have already dealt with the meaning of the first two Scriptures. The last mention in the Book of Revelation points to God's faithfulness towards the people of Israel. The temple of God is opened in heaven, and the ark of His covenant is seen in His temple. It is a heavenly vision, and the ark is symbolical of God's goodness in Christ. God thinks of His people and He is ready to bless them. His mercy is as ever centred in Christ, the true Ark of the covenant. In the end time He will remember His unconditional promises to the patriarchs and introduce His people into their long-awaited millennial blessings.

It is our privilege as believers to know that the **reality** is found in Christ. Therefore we do not need any **copies** of the things in the heavens (Heb. 9:23). May it be our constant desire then, to seek and to honour Him, as David and Solomon did with the ark of the covenant which spoke of Him.

No temple made with hands, His place of service is.
In heaven itself He stands, a heavenly Priesthood His.
In Him the shadows of the law,
Are all fulfilled and now withdraw.

Chapter Two Publications

Order Code

André, G.
123146	More Fruit, the Father's Loving Discipline, pb	£	1.25

Bouter, A.E.
113399	Behold, I Stand at the Door, pb	£	1.95
123203	Servants of God, pb	£	1.95

Bouter, H.
123028	Bethel, The Dwelling Place of the God of Jacob, pb, 2nd ed.	£	2.95
123046	Christ, the Wisdom of God, pb, 2nd ed.	£	1.25
123062	Divine Design, God's Plan of Salvation, pb	£	1.25
123107	In the Beginning (Genesis 1-11), pb	£	2.95
123112	Jacob's Last Words, pb, 2nd ed.	£	2.95
123114	John, the Beloved Disciple, pb, 2nd ed.	£	1.25
123185	Reflections on the Greatness of our Lord, pb, 2nd ed.	£	1.25
190069	The Healing of Naaman, pb	£	1.25

Bull, G.T.
123194	The Rock and the Sand, Glimpses of the Life of Faith, pb	£	5.95

Darby, J.N.
123170	Pilgrim Portions, pb	£	3.95

Deck, J.G.
123106	Hymns and Sacred Poems & brief biography, hb	£	3.95

Dennett, E.
123043	The Children of God, hb	£	8.95

Dronsfield, W.R.
123069	The Eternal Son of Father (2nd ed.), pb	£	1.30
123232	Unity and Authority (2nd printing), pb	£	1.30

Harris, J.L.
123015	Antinomianism & Legalism, pb (or, What is the Rule for Christian Conduct?)	£	1.80

Kelly, W.
123030	The Bible Treasury Magazine 1856/1920. 16 Vols. + Index	£	250.00
123078	F.E. Raven Heterodox on Eternal Life, hb	£	2.95
123191	The Revelation, Greek Text & Translation, hb	£	5.95
123059	Daniel's Seventy Weeks, pb	£	1.30
123118	The Lamentations of Jeremiah, hb	£	3.95
123247	Unity and Fellowship, pb	£	1.95

Koechlin, J.
123213   The Tabernacle   £   1.95
         (pullout folder in English, French, German and Spanish)
Lowe, W.J.
123151   A Nest in the Altar, hb   £   4.95
Mackintosh, C.H.
150094   Genesis to Deuteronomy – Notes on the Pentateuch, hb   £ 19.95
150076   Mackintosh Treasury, hb   £ 19.95
123021   The Assembly of God, pb   £   1.80
         (or, The All-sufficiency of the Name of Jesus)
123130   The Lord's Coming, pb   £   1.95
123002   Unity, What is it and am I confessing it? pb   £   0.75
Mair, G.
123079   The Fisherman's Gospel Manual, pb   £   3.95
Reid, Wm (MA)
123126   Literature & Mission of Plymouth Brethren, pb   £   0.75
Rossier, H.L.
123237   What is a Meeting of the Assembly? pb (new ed.)   £   1.80
Rouw, J.
123083   Gems Tell Their Secret, pb, full colour   £   2.25
123206   Here is the Smallest Bible in the World, with NCR slide   £   1.50
123104   House of Go(l)d–Welcome, pb   £   1.95
123204   Shalom and Israel, pb. full colour   £   2.25
Smith, H.
190051   Guidance in the Day of ruin, pb   £   2.95
Seibel, A.
123057   The Church Subtly Deceived, pb   £   3.95
Snell, H.H.
123004   The Way of Faith in an Evil Time (2nd printing) pb   £   1.95
Stuart, C.E.
123177   Primitive Christianity & the Sufficiency of the Word, hb   £   8.95
Turner, W.G.
123113   John Nelson Darby, a biography, latest ed., pb   £   4.50
Wallace, F.
123263   Spiritual Songsters, biographical sketches of
         Hymnwriters, hb   £   9.95
Wijnholds, H.
123038   Called to Fellowship, pb   £   1.95

Available from: Chapter Two Trust,
Fountain House, Conduit Mews, Woolwich, London, SE18 7AP, England
www.chaptertwo.org.uk, e-mail: chapter2uk@aol.com

The Chapter Two Trust is more a mission than a business. We exist to promote the Christian faith. If we can be of any help to you, please write. If the reading of this book has suggested any questions to your mind and you would like further contact, please do not hesitate to write to us.

We conduct free Bible Correspondence Courses. These have been designed to take you through the essential doctrines of the Christian faith. Write to us for the first paper of the Basic ten part course, we do not charge and you will be rewarded by a better knowledge of the Holy Bible.

Bible Correspondence Course Department
Chapter Two Trust
Fountain House
Conduit Mews
London SE18 7AP
United Kingdom

'Thy word is truth'
John 17:17